ENGLISH

Back to Basics

Classroom and Homework Activities

word study

punctuation

spelling

grammar

Jenni Harrold

6316UK

English – Back To Basics *(Yr 6/P 7)*

Published by R.I.C. Publications® 2010

Republished under licence by Prim-Ed Publishing 2010
Reprinted Prim-Ed Publishing 2014
Copyright© Jenni Harrold 2010
ISBN 978-1-84654-248-0
PR– 6316UK

Titles available in this series:
English – Back To Basics *(Yr 1/P 2)*
English – Back To Basics *(Yr 2/P 3)*
English – Back To Basics *(Yr 3/P 4)*
English – Back To Basics *(Yr 4/P 5)*
English – Back To Basics *(Yr 5/P 6)*
English – Back To Basics *(Yr 6/P 7)*
English – Back To Basics *(Yr 6 Ext/S 1)*

Internet websites
In some cases, websites or specific URLs may be recommended. While these are checked and rechecked at the time of publication, the publisher has no control over any subsequent changes which may be made to webpages. It is *strongly* recommended that the class teacher checks *all* URLs before allowing pupils to access them.

View all pages online

Website: www.prim-ed.com

Foreword

English – Back To Basics is a comprehensive resource designed to teach and revise basic literacy concepts. Essential skills are covered in spelling and word study, punctuation and grammar; with phonics included in Books Yr 1/P 2, Yr 2/P 3 and Yr 3/P 4. Each of the pages focuses on one concept, which is developed through relevant, graded activities.

Although intended as a homework series, these books are also ideal for:

- teaching a new concept
- consolidation
- assessment
- revision.

Titles in the series are:

English – Back To Basics – Yr 1/P 2
English – Back To Basics – Yr 2/P 3
English – Back To Basics – Yr 3/P 4
English – Back To Basics – Yr 4/P 5
English – Back To Basics – Yr 5/P 6
English – Back To Basics – Yr 6/P 7
English – Back To Basics – Yr 6 Ext/S 1

Contents

Format

This series of books contains pupil and teacher pages focusing on skills in the following areas:

- spelling and word study
- punctuation
- grammar
- phonics (Books Yr 1/P 2, Yr 2/P 3 and Yr 3/P 4).

Features

This series of books:

- provides activities on each page that relate to one literacy concept
- follows an organised format in which concepts are repeated and expanded across year levels
- uses a focal list of vocabulary
- has a pupil page supported by a corresponding teachers page
- has a teachers page that includes answers and detailed information explaining each concept
- provides additional reference information for teachers.

Purpose

This series of books is ideal for:

- teaching a new concept
- consolidating and revising knowledge and skills
- homework activities to revise skills taught in class
- assessment.

Spelling and vocabulary

There are two different lists of words used in each book:

- an age-appropriate spelling list of 40 words, and
- a high-frequency vocabulary list.

Both lists are used frequently throughout each book in the areas of spelling and word study, punctuation and grammar.

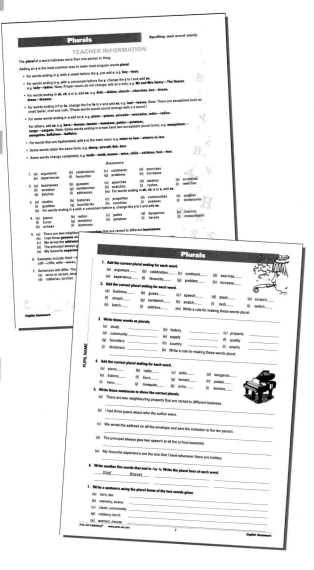

Additional reference material

This book includes:

- a word-building table which shows the base word, plural form, prefixes, suffixes, syllables, synonyms and antonyms
- an extensive glossary of terms used in spelling and word study, punctuation and grammar
- vowel sounds and the different ways they are represented
- consonant sounds and the different ways they are represented
- spelling rules
- prefixes, their meanings and examples
- suffixes, their meanings and examples
- word origins – Latin and Greek root words with their meanings and examples
- words commonly misspelt
- words easily confused or misused
- prepositions and prepositional phrases
- words that can be used as adjectives or adverbs.

Country/Subject/Level	Curriculum Objectives
England English Year Six	**Reading – Word Reading** • apply their growing knowledge of root words, prefixes and suffixes, both to read aloud and to understand the meaning of new words they meetText Structure and Organisation **Writing – Transcription – Spelling** • use further prefixes and suffixes and understand the guidance for adding them • spell some words with silent letters • continue to distinguish between homophones and other words which are often confused • use knowledge of morphology and etymology in spelling and understand that the spelling of some words needs to be learnt specifically **Writing – Vocabulary, Grammar and Punctuation** • using adverbs to indicate degrees of possibilities • using commas to clarify meaning or avoid ambiguity in writing • using hyphens to avoid ambiguity • using brackets, dashes or commas to indicate parenthesis • using semi-colons, colons or dashes to mark boundaries between independent clauses • using a colon to introduce a list
Northern Ireland Language and Literacy Key Stage Two	**Writing** • use a variety of skills to spell words correctly • develop increasing competence in the use of grammar and punctuation to create clarity of meaning
Republic of Ireland English Fifth Class	**Receptiveness to Language** • improve ability to recognise and understand words by using root words, prefixes, suffixes and syllabification **Competence and Confidence in Using Language** • understand the functions and know the names of the parts of speech • learn about and name the basic properties of nouns and verbs • become familiar with compound and complex sentences, and know and understand the terms 'phrase' and 'clause' • observe the conventions of grammar, punctuation and spelling
Scotland Literacy and English Second	**Second - Reading** • develop knowledge of punctuation and grammar to read texts **Second - Writing** • spell most words I need to communicate, using spelling rules • use appropriate punctuation, vary sentence structures and divide work into paragraphs
Wales English Key Stage Two	**Reading - Skills** • develop phonic, graphic and grammatical knowledge and word recognition • develop understanding of the structure, vocabulary, grammar and punctuation of English, and of how these clarify meaning **Writing - Skills** • use a range of sentence structures, linking them coherently and developing the ability to use paragraphs effectively • use punctuation to clarify meaning • choose and use appropriate vocabulary • use the standard forms of English: nouns, pronouns, adjectives, adverbs, prepositions, connectives and verb tenses

Spelling list

accident	celebrate	favourite	increase	practise	scene
afford	centre	future	judge	problem	separate
although	condition	government	luggage	quality	special
anxious	continue	guess	measure	recent	surround
argue	disappoint	honest	neighbour	regular	valuable
author	exercise	imagine	passenger	remember	
business	experience	immediately	position	rescue	

Vocabulary list

addition	describe	example	litre	parents	study
alphabet	difference	exercise	magazine	popular	subtraction
available	division	faction	meaning	predict	timetable
calculator	double	fraction	measurement	property	
capital	download	graph	mobile	question	
choice	enough	history	multiplication	range	
community	equal	journal	novel	sentence	
create	exact	language	paragraph	solve	

Spelling rules

Write *i* before *e*, except after *c*.

For example: friend, believe, receive, receipt

Some exceptions: foreign, either, science, weird, height, species

Write *ie* after *c* for words with a *shuhn* sound.

For example: sufficient, ancient, conscience, efficient

Write *ei* when the vowel sounds like an *a*.

For example: weigh, rein, reign, neighbour

For words ending in *y*:

- retain the **y** when adding **–ing**;
  for example: crying, studying

- retain the **y** if it is preceded by a vowel, when adding **s** or a suffix;
  for example: employs, employer

- change the **y** to *i* if it is preceded by a consonant, when adding a suffix;
  for example: cries, studies

Some exceptions: dryness, shyness.

Drop the final *e* to most words when adding a suffix beginning with a vowel

For example: use—usable
make—making

Double the consonant when adding a suffix starting with a vowel (e.g. -ing) to:

- a word of one syllable ending in a single consonant, preceded by a vowel;
  for example: drip—dripping
  sit—sitting

- a word of more than one syllable ending in a single consonant, preceded by a vowel **if** the stress is on the final syllable;
  for example: begin—beginning
  commit—committed.

When the stress is not on the final syllable, the single consonant remains;
for example: develop—developing—developed.

Exceptions include many words ending in *l*, where the *l* is always doubled;
for example: appal—appalling
travel—travelling.

Word	Base	Plural	Prefixes	Suffixes	Syllables	Synonym	Antonym
accident		accidents		ly al	ac-ci-dent	mishap	
afford			un(able)	ed ing able	af-ford		
although	though				al-though		
anxious				ly ness	an-xious	nervous	calm
argue			un(able)	ed ing able ly	ar-gue	disagree	agree
author		authors		ed ial ing less	au-thor	writer	
business		businesses			bus(i)ness	company	
celebrate				ed ing ion or ory	cel-e-brate	commemorate	
centre		centres	un(ed) re	ed ing able	cen-tre	middle	
condition		conditions	un(ed)	ed ing aly al	con-di-tion	state	
continue			dis(ed)	ed ing ment	con-tin-ue	persist	discontinue
disappoint				ed ing ment	dis-ap-point	upset	please
exercise		exercises		able ed ing er	ex-er-cise	train	
experience		experiences	un(ed)	ed ing	ex-per-i-ence	knowledge	
favourite	favour	favourites			fa-vour-ite	preferred	disliked
future		futures		ist	fu-ture	outlook	past
government	govern	governments		al ally	gov-ern-ment	administration	
guess		guesses		able ed er ing	guess	estimate	certainty
honest			dis	ly	hon-est	true	dishonest
imagine	image		un(able)	able ation ed er ing	i-ma-gine	dream	
immediately	immediate				im-med-i-ate-ly	now	later
increase		increases	un(ed)	able ed ing	in-crease	rise	decrease
judge		judges	mis	ed er ing ment ship	judge	determine	
luggage	lug	luggage			lug-gage	baggage	
measure		measures	un(able)	able ed ing ment	mea-sure	calculate	
neighbour		neighbours		ing ly	neigh-bour		
passenger	passage	passengers			pas-sen-ger	traveller	
position	posit	positions		al ed ing	pos-i-tion	place	
practise				ed ing	prac-tise	train	
problem		problems		atic	prob-lem	puzzle	solution
quality		qualities			qual-i-ty	excellence	inferiority
recent				ly ness	re-cent	current	dated
regular		regulars		ity ly	reg-u-lar	usual	irregular
remember				ed er ing	re-mem-ber	recall	forget
rescue		rescues		ed er ing	res-cue	save	
scene		scenes		ery ic	scene	setting	
separate				ed ing ness	sep-ar-ate	divide	connect
special		specials		ity	spe-cial	unique	ordinary
surround	round			ed ing	sur-round	enclose	
valuable	value	valuables	in	ness	val-u-a-ble	worthy	worthless

Spelling and word study

Abbreviation

An abbreviation is a word written in shortened form. A full stop may be used to show part of the word is missing. However, if the last letter of the word is used, there is no full stop.

For example: *Mon.* for Monday
Dr for Doctor

Acronym

A word made up from the initial letters of a phrase.

For example: *SIDS* (sudden infant death syndrome)
radar (radio detecting and ranging)

(Note: If it is not pronounced as a word, it is an intialism; e.g. *LPG*.)

Antonyms

Words that are opposite in meaning.

For example: *hot/cold*
dark/light
wet/dry

Base word

The root word or main part of the word. Prefixes and suffixes can be added to the base word.

For example: *read*ing, mis*guid*ed, *care*fully

Compound word

Two or more words joined together.

For example: *pancake, teaspoon, underground*

Consonant

Any letter of the alphabet that is not a vowel.

For example: *b, c, d, f, g, h, j*

Contraction

A shortened form of a word. An apostrophe is used to replace the deleted letters.

For example: *I'm, we're, they'll, she'd, can't*

Derivative

A word made from adding prefixes and suffixes to a base word.

For example: *sleep*ing, un*usual*, *happ*ily

Digraph

Two letters representing one phoneme.

For example: *th, sh, wh, er, ck, ou*

Eponyms

Eponyms are words that come from a person's name or name of a place.

For example: Jules *Leotard*
Anders *Celsius*
Earl of *Cardigan*

Etymology

The study of the origin and history of words.

For example: *annual* from the Latin word *annu*, meaning 'year'

Grapheme

The written representation of a sound.

For example: *ew, ing, th*

Homographs

Words that are spelt the same but have different origins and meanings and are sometimes pronounced differently.

For example: *cricket, wind*

Homophones

Words that sound the same but are spelled differently.

For example: *peace/piece*
threw/through
bored/board

Morpheme

The smallest unit of meaning.

For example: *house/keep/ing*

Phoneme

The smallest unit of sound in a word that can be represented by one, two, three or four letters. There are 44 phonemes in English.

For example: *t*o, sh*oe*, thr*ough*

Phonetics

System of spelling words that represents sounds by symbols.

Plural

Indicates more than one person or thing.

For example: two *books*
three *wishes*
four *children*

Prefix

Used at the beginning of a base word to change meaning.

For example: *in*edible, *un*conscious, *il*legal, *dis*obey

Singular

Only one person or thing.

For example: one *book*, a *table*, an *apple*

Suffix

Used at the end of a base word.

For example: work*ing*, lone*ly*, walk*ed*, edit*or*

Syllable

A unit of sound which contains a vowel sound. All words are made up of one or more syllables.

For example: talk, nerv-ous, in-de-pen-dent

Synonyms

Words that are similar in meaning.

For example: *big/large*
small/tiny
wet/damp

Thesaurus

A reference book which groups words by meaning.

For example: *promise*—pledge, guarantee, engagement, commit, assure, secure

Trigraph

Three letters representing one phoneme.

For example: *high*, fu*dge*, p*ear*

Vowel

The five letters of the alphabet that are not consonants.

These are: *a, e, i, o* and *u*.

Punctuation

Apostrophe

Used to show ownership and in contractions to show where letters have been dropped.

For example: Jackie's dog wasn't barking.

Capital letters

Used to start a sentence, as the first letter of proper nouns, for the pronoun *I*, in titles, and to start direct speech.

Colon

Used to introduce additional information.

For example: Use the following: eggs, bacon, milk, salt and pepper.

Comma

Used as a short pause to separate parts of a sentence and items in a list.

For example: The boy, a great athlete, was competing in most events.

I took pens, pencils, paper and paints to the class.

Dash

Used to provide additional information or show that something is unfinished.

For example: I opened the gift—it was just what I wanted.

Ellipsis

Used to mark letters or words that have been left out and a pause or interruption

For example: Her birthday party was wonderful … the best ever!

Exclamation mark

Used to show strong emotion.

For example: That's fantastic news!

Forward slash

Used to show options, shortened forms, in web addresses and instead of *per*, *an* or *a*.

For example: *true/false*

60km/h

Full stop

Used at the end of a sentence or in some abbreviations.

For example: His birthday was on 21 Feb.

Hyphen

Used to join words and word parts, clarify meaning and divide words at the end of a line.

For example: *re-signed* a contract

brother-in-law

three-quarters

Parentheses

Used to enclose additional information such as a comment, explanation or example.

For example: Tia (my sister) showed me how to use the program.

Question mark

Used at the end of a sentence to show a question to be answered.

For example: Did you finish everything you wanted to?

Quotation marks

Used to indicate direct speech, quotations and specific titles.

For example: 'Did you know the Spanish word "siesta" means a short nap?' Ben asked.

Semicolon

Used to separate short, balanced and linked phrases or clauses. It is stronger than a comma, not as strong as a full stop. It can also be used to separate items in a list of phrases or clauses.

For example: I bought new shoes; they were on sale.

I need 12 pens, pencils and rulers; 24 books, six erasers and two bags.

Grammar

Abstract noun

A word which describes things that cannot actually be heard, seen, smelt or tasted.

For example: *anger, beauty, danger, jealousy, loyalty, pain*

Active voice

The voice of the verb which shows that the subject of the sentence is performing the action.

For example: Her friend *drove* the car.

The dog *frightened* the child.

Adjective

A describing word used to add meaning to a noun or pronoun.

For example: He wore a *blue* shirt.

The meal was *delicious*.

Adverb

Adds meaning to a verb, adjective or other adverb. It can tell how, where or when.

For example: He worked *carefully*.

Yesterday, they walked to school.

She *finally* finished.

Agreement

Shows that linked words or phrases agree in terms of case, number, gender and person.

For example: *He is* welcome. *They are* welcome.

She tried to write the story *herself*.

Article

A subclass of determiners where *a* and *an* are indefinite and *the* is definitive.

For example: *a* computer, *an* apple, *the* dog

Auxiliary verb

A 'helping' verb that is used in forming tense, mood and voices with other verbs. The verbs *to be, to have* and *to do* are often used as auxiliary verbs.

For example: I *was* thinking of you.

He *does* leave his room in a mess.

We *have* seen it.

Clause

A group of words with a subject and its verb.

For example: *She walked to the station.*

Collective noun

A group of persons or things.

For example: a *class* of pupils, a *flock* of sheep, a *herd* of elephants

Command verb (imperative)

A verb used as an order or command.

For example: *Stop* talking so loudly.

Common noun

A word naming general rather than particular things.

For example: *apple, river, table, colour*

Complex sentence

Has a main (independent) clause and at least one subordinate (dependent) clause.

For example: I like swimming before I walk along the beach.

Compound sentence

Has two or more independent clauses with a linking word.

For example: The nurse worked hard and helped the sick child.

Conjunction

A joining word for words, phrases, clauses and sentences.

For example: I ate an apple *and* a pear.

I was tired *but* I had to work *because* the assignment was due.

Connective

A connecting word that tells order and what is coming next.

For example: I'll finish the dishes *first* and *then* watch a film.

Determiner

A word that is used in front of a noun or pronoun to tell something about it.

For example: *a* tiger, *the* tiger, *some* tigers, *both* tigers, *that* tiger, *three* tigers

Direct speech

Exactly what is spoken, enclosed in quotation marks.

For example: *'Are you feeling thirsty?'* she asked.

Double negative

When two negatives are used together, with the effect of cancelling each other so the negative meaning is lost.

For example: She was*n't* doing *nothing*.

He did*n't* get *no* lunch.

Finite verb

A verb that has a subject. A finite verb must be a part of every sentence and agree with its subject.

For example: The ball *rolls*.

The balls *roll*.

Idiom

A phrase that is not meant literally.

For example: *over the moon*

frog in my throat

Grammar

Indefinite pronoun

A pronoun that refers to people or things generally and not specifically.

For example: *anybody, anything, everybody, everyone, somebody, something*

Indirect speech

Reports, and often alters, direct speech without the use of quotes.

For example: I asked her to be quiet.
She told me she would leave early.

Main (independent) clause

A group of words that can stand alone and make sense without being dependent on any other part of a sentence.

For example: *I decided to go shopping* after I had my lunch.

Modifier

A word or group of words that affect the meaning of another word in some way by giving more information. They might describe, define or make a meaning more precise.

For example: The TV is in the *largest* room.

Bright-eyed and inquisitive, the squirrel searched for food.

Noun

A word that names a person, place, thing, feeling or idea.

For example: doctor, Paris, suitcase, fear, courage

Object

Shows what or whom the verb affects.

For example: They purchased a *house*.
She wore *blue jeans*.

Paragraph

A group of sentences that are about one main idea. The sentences should follow in a logical order.

Passive voice

The voice of the verb which shows that the subject is having an action done to it.

For example: Max *was tickled* by his sister.
She *was surprised* by the visitors.

Person

Text may be written as the first, second or third person and is indicated by the use of pronouns and verbs.

For example: *I* wrote the book.
It must be *yours*.
Did *he* write the book?

Personal pronoun

Used in place of a person.

First person personal pronouns are: *I, me, mine, we, us, ours*.

Second person personal pronouns are: *you, yours*.

Third person personal pronouns are: *he, his, him, she, hers, her, it, its, they, them, theirs*.

Phrase

A group of words in a sentence which does not contain a finite verb.

For example: She walked *towards the house*.
The car crashed *into the tree*.

Possessive pronoun

A pronoun used to show ownership.

For example: That book is *his*.
I think it's *hers*.
I have *mine* here.
It must be *yours*.

Predicate

What is written or said about the subject of a sentence.

For example: The teacher was *tired and hungry*.
The kitchen was *clean and tidy*.

Preposition

Used in front of a noun or pronoun to describe the relationship.

For example: *under* the water, *to* him, *at* the concert, *before* lunch, *around* them

Pronoun

Used in place of a noun to reduce repetition.

For example: Peter is conscientious. *He* works quietly.

Proper noun

Used to specifically name a person or thing.

For example: *Jemma, Antarctica, Sahara Desert*

Relative pronoun

Used to connect or relate one part of a sentence to another.

For example: Here is the house *that* I want to buy.
I met the man *whose* story I had read.

Sentence

A group of words that makes sense on its own. It may have one or more clauses. It must have a finite verb, a capital letter at the start and end in a full stop, question mark or exclamation mark.

For example: *I'll eat breakfast after I've had a shower*.

Simple sentence

A sentence with only one verb (part of the predicate) and one subject.

For example: *I played a game*.
They ate dinner together.

Slang

Words or phrases in common use that are not considered to be part of standard English.

For example: *aggro, dude*.

Statement

A sentence which states a fact.

For example: *We will not be leaving today*.

Grammar

Subject

The person or thing who is doing the action in a sentence.

For example: *Mrs Green* taught music.

The *football team* won the game with the last kick.

Subordinate (dependent) clause

A group of words that cannot stand alone and make sense. It is dependent on the main clause for its meaning.

For example: I ate everything on the plate *because I was hungry.*

Tense

Verb tenses tell whether the action is happening in the past, present or future.

For example: I *walked*, I *walk*, I *am walking*, I *will walk*.

Verb

An action or state of being word.

For example: She *read* the book.

He *has written* a story.

They *will eat* dinner.

We *thought* about it.

Additional word lists

Words used as prepositions

aboard	among	beyond	in	over	under
about	around	but	inside	past	until
above	at	by	into	per	up
across	before	concerning	like	round	upon
after	behind	despite	near	since	via
against	below	down	of	through	with
along	beneath	during	off	throughout	within
alongside	beside	except	on	till	without
amid	besides	for	onto	to	
amidst	between	from	out	towards	

Prepositional phrases

according to	aside from	behind in	in front of	in regard to	on account of
ahead of	as to	due to	in lieu of	in spite of	on board
apart from	back of	in addition to	in light of	instead of	out of
as far as	because of	in the back of	in place of	in view of	owing to

Words used as adjectives or adverbs

bad	doubtless	fast	loose	right	straight
better	early	first	loud	rough	third
bright	enough	hard	low	second	tight
cheap	even	high	much	sharp	well
close	fair	late	near	slow	worse
deep	far	little	quick	smooth	wrong

Vowel sounds

There are 19 vowel sounds listed below. Most of these vowel sounds can be written in a number of different ways. The letters used to represent sounds in words are called 'graphemes'.

Knowledge about common graphemes and an understanding of how to use them when selecting the particular one needed to spell a word correctly, are essential spelling skills.

Some of the most commonly used graphemes for each vowel sound are found in the table below.

Sound	Graphemes
'a' as in bat	a (cat)
'a' as in rain	ai (pain) ay (tray) a-e (plate) a (baby) ea (break) ei (rein) ey (grey)
'ar' as in bar	ar (car) a (class) al (calf) au (laugh)
'air' as in pair	air (chair) are (care) ear (bear) ere (there) eir (their)
'aw' as in paw	aw (yawn) or (fork) au (sauce) a (ball) ore (store) oar (roar) oor (poor) ough (fought) augh (caught) al (walk)
'e' as in tell	e (jet) ea (spread)
'ee' as in tree	ee (sheep) ea (beat) y (funny) ie (thief) ei (ceiling) ey (key) i (ski) e-e (athlete)
'er' as in fern	er (germ) ir (girl) ur (purse) or (word) ear (earn) our (journey)
'ear' as in appear	ear (near) eer (deer) ere (here) ier (tier)
'i' as in bit	i (fin) y (pyramid) ui (build)
'i' as in hive	i (find) ie (pie) y (sky) i-e (fine) igh (sigh)
'o' as in top	o (clot) a (wasp) au (sausage) ou (cough)
'o' as in hope	o (no) oa (boat) oe (toe) ow (slow) o-e (home)
'ow' as in cow	ow (down) ou (loud)
'oy' as in toy	oy (boy) oi (coin)
'oo' as in cook	oo (book) u (bush) ou (should)
'oo' as in boot	oo (spoon) ew (flew) ue (true) ou (soup) ui (fruit) o (to)
'u' as in mud	u (truck) o (some) ou (young)
'yu' as in use	u-e (fuse) u (duty) ew (new) ue (avenue) eau (beauty)

There are 25 consonant sounds listed below. Most of these consonant sounds can be written in a number of different ways. The letters used to represent sounds in words are called 'graphemes'.

Knowledge about common graphemes and an understanding of how to use them when selecting the particular one needed to spell a word correctly, are essential spelling skills.

Some of the most commonly used graphemes for each consonant sound are found in the table below.

Sound	*Graphemes*
'b' as in big	b (bat) bb (rabbit)
'c' as in cat	c (clean) ck (pack) ch (school) k (kite) cc (occupy) que (cheque)
'ch' as in chin	ch (church) tch (watch)
'd' as in dog	d (doll) dd (rudder) ed (talked)
'f' as in fat	f (fed) ff (giraffe) ph (phone) gh (laugh)
'g' as in get	g (goat) gg (egg) gu (guide) gh (ghost)
'h' as in hat	h (have) wh (who)
'j' as in jam	j (jet) g (giant) dge (hedge) gg (suggest)
'l' as in look	l (lot) ll (hill) le (little)
'm' as in met	m (mother) mm (hammer) mb (climb) lm (calm) mn (autumn)
'n' as in now	n (nurse) nn (runner) kn (knot)
'ng' as in sing	ng (strong) n (sink)
'p' as in pot	p (pin) pp (ripped)
'r' as in run	r (red) rr (carry) wr (write)
's' as in sat	s (sun) ss (toss) c (cent) ce (rice) sc (scene)
'sh' as in ship	sh (sheep) s (sugar) ss (pressure) ch (machine) ci (special) ti (station) si (tension)
't' as in tap	t (tent) tt (written) th (Thomas) ed (cooked)
'th' as in thin	th (think)
'th' as in then	th (that) the (breathe)
'v' as in van	v (vase) f (of)
'w' as in was	w (watch) wh (when)
'x' as in box	x (fox) cks (socks)
'y' as in yes	y (yell)
'z' as in zebra	z (zip) zz (fizz) s (has)
'zh' as in measure	s (treasure) si (television)

Prefix	Meaning	Example(s)
anti-	opposed, against	**anti**septic
bi-	two, twice	**bi**cycle
bio-	life	**bio**graphy
circum-	around	**circum**ference
co-	together	**co**operate
contra-	opposite, against	**contra**dict
de-	away, from, down	**de**fer, **de**scend
dis-	apart	**dis**connect
en- em-	make	**en**able, **em**brace
ex-	former	**ex**-premier
for-	not	**for**get
fore-	before	**fore**cast
giga-	billion	**giga**byte
hyper-	over, exclusive	**hyper**active
il-	not	**il**legal
in-	not, in	**in**complete, **in**side
im- ir-	not	**im**possible, **ir**regular
inter-	between, among	**inter**view
mal-	wrong	**mal**function
mega-	million	**mega**byte
micro-	small	**micro**scope
milli-	thousand	**milli**litre
mini-	small	**mini**skirt
mis-	wrongly	**mis**judge
non-	not	**non**sense
out-	outside, detached	**out**patient
post-	after	**post**graduate
pre-	before	**pre**heat
re-	again, back	**re**peat, **re**turn
semi-	half	**semi**circle
sub-	under	**sub**marine
super-	over, above	**super**human
trans-	across	**trans**port
tri-	three, triple	**tri**cycle
un-	not	**un**done
uni-	one, single	**uni**form
with-	against, away	**with**hold

Suffixes

Suffix	Meaning	Example(s)
-able, -ible	capable of, for	adapt**able**, poss**ible**
-al, -ical	of, relating to	matern**al**, mag**ical**
-ar	like	circul**ar**
-ate	to make	aggrav**ate**
-ation	act of	invit**ation**
-dom	state of	free**dom**
-er, -or	one who	farm**er**, act**or**
-ess	feminine of nouns	princ**ess**
-fold	number of parts, times	two**fold**
-ful	able to, full of	help**ful**, plate**ful**
-ion	action, state, quality	considerat**ion**, promot**ion**
-ise	make into	human**ise**
-ish	belonging, like	girl**ish**, Swed**ish**
-ism	state, quality, act of	hero**ism**, bapt**ism**
-ist	one who	art**ist**
-ive	like, connected with	nat**ive**, protect**ive**
-less	without	child**less**
-ly	like, how, when	man**ly**, dark**ly**, year**ly**
-ment	result, state, quality of	achieve**ment**, judg**ment**
-ous	full of	nerv**ous**
-phobia	fear, dread	claustro**phobia**

LATIN ROOT WORDS

Root word	Meaning	Example(s)
scribe	writing	de**scribe**, in**scribe**, **scrib**ble, pre**scribe**, tran**scribe**
port	carry	trans**port**, **port**able, re**port**, ex**port**, im**port**, sup**port**
ped	foot	**ped**estrian, **ped**al, **ped**estal, im**ped**e, ex**ped**ition
spire	breathe	in**spire**, con**spire**, re**spire**, tran**spire**
mit	send, let go	trans**mit**, o**mit**, ad**mit**, per**mit**, re**mit**
fact	make, do	manu**fact**ure, **fact**or, **fact**ion, satis**fact**ion, **fact**ory
duc, duce, duct	to lead	con**duct**, intro**duce**, pro**duce**, e**duc**ate, con**duct**or
cap, capit	head	**cap**ital, **cap**tain, de**capit**ate, **capit**ulate
flu	flow	**flu**id, **flu**ent, in**flu**ence, af**flu**ent, ef**flu**ent
mani, manu	hand	**manu**al, **manu**facture, **manu**script, **mani**pulate
aqua, aque	water	**aqua**tic, **aqua**rium, **aqua**plane, **aque**duct, **Aqua**rius
aud	hear	**aud**io, **aud**ience, **aud**ible, **aud**ition
anni, annu	year	**annu**al, **anni**versary, bi**annu**al, **annu**ity
bene	well	**bene**fit, **bene**ficial, **bene**factor, **bene**ficiary, **bene**volent
prem, prim	first	**prim**ary, **prim**e, **prim**itive, **prim**er, **prem**ier
unus	one	**un**it
duo	two	**du**et
tres	three	**tri**angle
quatuor	four	**quar**ter
quinque	five	**quin**tet
sex	six	**sex**tuplet
septum	seven	**Sept**ember (7th month on Roman calendar)
octo	eight	**octo**pus
novem	nine	**Novem**ber (9th month on Roman calendar)
decem	ten	**dec**imal
centum	hundred	**cent**ury
mille	thousand	**milli**metre

GREEK ROOT WORDS

Root word	Meaning	Example(s)
meter, metre	measure	centi**metre**, milli**metre**, thermo**meter**, baro**meter**, pedo**meter**, speedo**meter**
micro	small	**micro**scopic, **micro**scope, **micro**phone
aero	air	**aero**naut, **aer**ate, **aero**plane, **aer**ial
sphere	globe, ball	atmo**sphere**, strato**sphere**, hemi**sphere**
tele	far off	**tele**phone, **tele**port, **tele**vise, **tele**vision
logy	word, knowledge, science of	psycho**logy**, bio**logy**, zoo**logy**, neuro**logy**
auto	self	**auto**matic, **auto**biography, **auto**graph, **auto**mobile
logos	word, reason	**log**ic, **log**istic, **log**ical

LIST 1

about	choose	friend	none	their
ache	colour	guess	ocean	though
address	coming	half	often	through
afraid	cough	heard	once	together
again	could	hospital	people	tomorrow
agree	country	hour	picture	tonight
almost	couple	hungry	piece	touch
always	cousin	important	please	trouble
among	daughter	insect	promise	Tuesday
answer	decide	instead	question	uncle
any	definite	interesting	quick	used
around	different	invite	ready	useful
August	difficult	January	reason	vegetable
aunt	discuss	knew	remember	voice
autumn	doctor	know	rough	Wednesday
balloon	does	lately	said	welcome
beautiful	don't	laugh	separate	where
because	done	library	September	which
been	during	listen	sign	who
beginning	early	lose	since	women
behaviour	easy	making	some	won't
bicycle	eight	many	someone	would
breakfast	every	meant	special	write
built	exercise	message	spread	writing
business	famous	might	straight	wrong
busy	February	minute	strange	wrote
buy	finish	naughty	sure	yesterday
careful	forgotten	nearly	surprise	

LIST 2

accident	customer	incident	private
adventure	damage	information	procedure
aeroplane	decoration	injury	punishment
altogether	delicious	instrument	pure
ambulance	disappointing	intelligent	pyjamas
amusing	discovery	jealous	quantity
anxious	disgraceful	knowledge	reasonable
appear	distract	lawyer	recreation
appreciate	division	league	religion
argument	doubt	machine	repair
assembly	election	material	request
association	electric	medicine	scarce
athlete	enormous	migrate	separate
attendance	enough	multiplication	serious
audience	excitement	museum	silence
author	extreme	musical	skilful
automatic	failure	mystery	subtraction
avenue	fashion	necessary	support
awful	favourite	neighbour	surround
balance	finally	nephew	technology
believe	forty	nervous	unknown
careless	frequent	niece	valuable
celebrate	generous	opinion	variety
centre	gradual	oxygen	visitor
certain	heritage	parliament	weary
chocolate	hesitate	passenger	weight
comfortable	honest	permission	weird
committee	horrible	persuade	yacht
conversation	imagination	physical	youth
curtain	immediately	population	

LIST 3

accessories	convenient	foreigner	irrelevant	outrageous	silhouette
acquaintance	cooperate	fortunately	irreplaceable	paralyse	sincerely
acquire	courageous	freight	irresponsible	participant	sophisticated
admittance	curious	fugitive	itinerary	permitted	spaghetti
adolescence	deceased	furious	jewellery	phenomenon	spontaneous
anniversary	definite	gauge	kidnapped	pneumonia	statistics
anonymous	desperate	genuine	knowledgeable	politician	successful
appalling	diabetes	glamorous	labelled	possession	sufficient
Arctic	diarrhoea	government	legendary	possibility	supervisor
assistance	difference	grammar	limousine	professional	surgeon
asthmatic	disappearance	grieve	maintenance	pronunciation	suspicious
basically	disapproval	guarantee	manageable	prosecute	technique
bouquet	disastrous	guard	manually	protein	therapeutic
boutique	discipline	hallucination	millionaire	questionnaire	tragedy
bureau	discrimination	harass	miraculous	queue	transferred
campaign	discussion	hereditary	mortgage	reassurance	twelfth
casualty	disease	hilarious	muscle	rebellious	unanimous
cautious	disinfectant	humorous	mysterious	receipt	unconscious
cemetery	distinguish	hypothetical	nausea	recommend	unique
chauffeur	documentary	hysterical	negotiate	referee	unnecessary
choreography	economically	ignorance	numerous	regretted	vaccinate
coincidence	efficient	illiterate	nutritious	rehabilitation	vague
colleague	eightieth	imaginative	obedient	relevant	visibility
commercial	electrician	immaculate	obese	responsibility	volunteered
commitment	embarrass	inappropriate	obscene	restaurant	vulnerable
communicate	encourage	independence	obsessive	resuscitate	wintry
competitive	escalator	indigenous	occasion	rhythm	worshipped
concussion	essential	ineligible	occurred	rumour	
congratulations	eventually	ingredient	offence	satellite	
conscientious	fascinate	inseparable	omitted	schedule	
conscious	fatigue	intermediate	opportunity	siege	
controversial	fierce	interrupt	ordinary	significant	

LIST 1

Words	Examples
angel/angle	We put the angel on the Christmas tree. A triangle might have a right angle.
as/like	I did as I was told. I was like my sister.
ate/eaten	I ate breakfast. I have eaten breakfast.
beat/beaten	We will beat them. We should have beaten them.
became/become	She became a star. She will become a star.
began/begun	He began the work. He has begun to work.
been/being	I have been to school. I like being at school.
beside/besides	I stood beside him. Who, besides your dad, is home?
blew/blown	The wind blew. The papers have blown away.
breath/breathe	He took a deep breath. He can breathe deeply.
can/may/might	She can do that. May I do that? I may do that. I might be able to do that.
came/come	She came late. They will come later.
chose/choose	I chose the apple. I will choose an apple.
dairy/diary	The milk came from the dairy. He wrote in his diary.
desert/dessert	The desert was dry. He deserted them. We had ice-cream for dessert.
did/done	He did the work. He has done the work.
forgot/forgotten	She forgot the number. He has forgotten to bring it.
gave/give	She gave me the book. I will give you the book.
gone/went	He has gone to school. She went to school.
hid/hidden	Mum hid the Christmas presents. The presents were hidden from us.
its/it's	The dog is wagging its tail. It's a sunny day.
knew/know/known	I knew the teacher. I know who she is. I wish I had known before.
laid/lain	It was laid on the table. It had lain on the table for a while.
learn/teach	I had to learn the words. She can teach me how to do it.
lend/borrow	I will lend you the book. Can I borrow the book?
loose/lose	These trousers feel loose. Don't lose your phone.
meter/metre	The meter was running. It was a metre long.
of/off	I was tired of working. I took off my hat.
outdoor/outdoors	Cricket is an outdoor sport. We played it outdoors.
passed/past	I passed the test. I walked past her.
practice/practise	He is going to football practice. He will practise his skills.
principal/principle	She is the principal of the school. She followed a basic principle.
quiet/quite	I was very quiet. It was quite funny.
rapt/wrapped	I was rapt with the result. I wrapped a present.
risen/rose	The sun had risen before I woke. The sun rose before I did.
role/roll	She played the role of a doctor. She ate a salad roll for lunch.
showed/shown	I showed her where I lived. He has shown me the way to go.
storey/story	They lived on the top storey of the building. I read the story.
their/there/they're	That is their house. They live there. They're going out.
threw/through	I threw the ball. I walked through the room.
tore/torn	He tore the shirt he was wearing. The shirt is torn.
wear/where/we're	I will wear the dress. Where are you? We're going to school.
went/gone	They went an hour ago. They have already gone.
who/which	I have two brothers who are older. I have two kittens which are cute.
who's/whose	Who's leaving now? Do you know whose dog it is?

LIST 2

Words	Examples
accept/except	Please accept this gift. Everyone went except Drew.
addition/edition	I completed the addition problems. There is a new edition of that book.
advice/advise	She asked for my advice. I would advise you to finish it.
affect/effect	She was affected by the news. It had a good effect on her
amend/emend	They should amend the rule. He needs to emend (edit) his work.
ballet/ballot	Her ballet dress was beautiful. We needed a ballot paper to vote.
belief/believe	My belief is that you will do well. I believe you will win.
charted/chartered	He charted the data. He chartered a boat for the day.
continual/continuous	She was in continual pain. It was a continuous line.
councillor/counsellor	The local councillor approved the plans. The counsellor listened to her.
dependant/dependent	The woman had two dependants. The child was dependent on her mother.
device/devise	The electronic device was expensive. She had to devise a new plan.
elicit/illicit	He tried to elicit information. The drug was illicit.
eligible/legible	The school was eligible for the grant. Her writing was legible.
emigrant/immigrant	The emigrant left his country. The immigrant arrived in his new country.
emission/omission	There was a gas emission. The omission of her name was an oversight.
employee/employer	The new employee worked hard. The boss was their employer.
forgave/forgiven	I easily forgave my best friend. I told her she was forgiven.
formally/formerly	I was dressed formally. I was formerly at another address.
human/humane	He is a human being. They had to treat the animal in a humane way.
licence/license	He had a driver's licence. He had to license the car.
mediate/meditate	She had to mediate between the groups. I took time to meditate and relax.
mistaken/mistook	I was mistaken about the time. I mistook the time it would take.
overtaken/overtook	They had overtaken the slow car. They overtook the car.
premier/premiere	The premier is the state leader. We went to the film premiere.
proof/prove	You need the right proof first. You will have to prove it's true.
refuge/refugee	He took refuge from the storm. The refugee arrived from another country.
review/revue	Write a review of the book. The musical revue was very funny.
scared/scarred	I was scared of the dark. The burn scarred my skin.
scraped/scrapped	She scraped her knee when she fell. I scrapped the work I was doing.
stationary/stationery	The train was stationary. The stationery included pencils.
suit/suite	He wore the new suit to the party. We stayed in an expensive hotel suite.
summary/summery	The summary was very brief. It was a fine, summery day.

TEACHER INFORMATION AND PUPIL PAGES

TEACHER INFORMATION

This list of 20 words forms part of the vocabulary consistently used throughout the book. The activities revise concepts previously introduced at other levels.

Answers

1. rescue, continue, argue
    Sentences will vary.

2. (a) accident—a, dent, den
    (b) disappoint—sap, point, in, is, appoint
    (c) passenger—pass, ass, as
    (d) surround—round
    (e) rescue—cue
    (f) valuable—able
    (g) position—posit, sit, it, on
    (h) immediately—mediate, media, ate, at

3. Answers may vary.
    (a) special   (b) valuable   (c) argue
    (d) anxious   (e) problem   (f) condition

4. afford, passenger, disappoint, luggage, accident, surround, business, immediately

5. Answers may include:
    passenger, rescue, quality, accident, luggage, position, problem, condition, business

6. (a) quality   (b) although   (c) practise
    (d) position   (e) continue   (f) afford

7. accident, afford, although, anxious, argue,
    business, condition, continue, disappoint, immediately,
    luggage, passenger, position, practise, problem,
    quality, rescue, special, surround, valuable

8. Sentences may vary.
    (a) business—one's affairs or occupation, a company
    (b) position—way, where thing is played, to place, rank or status

9. Answers may differ.
    (a) argu**ed**   (b) accident**ly**   (c) condition**ing**
    (d) problem**atic**   (e) disappoint**ment** (f) anxious**ness**

10. (a) condition   (b) value   (c) afford
    (d) round   (e) rescue   (f) special

| afford | passenger | rescue | practise | disappoint | continue | quality | luggage | position | anxious |
| valuable | accident | surround | problem | condition | argue | business | although | immediately | special |

1. Write the words that have *ue*. Show the meaning of each word in a sentence.

_____   _____

_____   _____

_____   _____

2. Write the small words in each of the following.

(a) accident _____   (b) disappoint _____   (c) passenger _____

(d) surround _____   (e) rescue _____   (f) valuable _____

(g) position _____   (h) immediately _____

3. Write the word that means:

(a) unique _____   (b) priceless _____   (c) disagree _____

(d) nervous _____   (e) puzzle _____   (f) state _____

4. Write the words with double letters.

_____

5. Write six words that can be nouns.

_____

6. Unscramble these.

(a) uaitqly _____   (b) ouhhglta _____   (c) raiesctp _____

(d) iioopstn _____   (e) eunitnoc _____   (f) orfdaf _____

7. Write the words in alphabetical order.

_____   _____   _____   _____

_____   _____   _____   _____

_____   _____   _____   _____

_____   _____   _____   _____

8. These words have more than one meaning. Write two sentences showing a different meaning for each word.

(a) business   _____

_____

(b) position   _____

_____

9. Add a different suffix to each word. *-ed -ment -ness -ly -ing -atic*

(a) argue _____   (b) accident _____   (c) condition _____

(d) problem _____   (e) disappoint_____   (f) anxious _____

10. Write the base word for each.

(a) unconditionally_____   (b) invaluable _____   (c) affordability _____

(d) surrounded _____   (e) rescuing _____   (f) speciality _____

PUPIL NAME

TEACHER INFORMATION

This list of 20 words forms part of the vocabulary consistently used throughout the book. The activities revise concepts previously introduced at other levels.

Answers

1. author, celebrate, centre, exercise, experience, favourite, future, government, guess, honest, increase, imagine, judge, measure, neighbour, recent, regular, remember, scene, separate

2. (a) regular, remember, neighbour, measure, centre, future, author
   (b) *ar, er, or, our, re, ure*

3. Answers will vary. Meanings are:
   (a) centre—middle   a place (e.g. recreation centre)
   (b) exercise—to move physically   an activity to do (maths exercise)
   (c) regular—consistent   the norm, average
   (d) experience—personal observation   an incident
   (e) judge—to decide (v.)   an official presiding over a court room (n.)

4. (a) honest   (b) author   (c) recent
   (d) guess   (e) scene   (f) imagine

5. (a) future   (b) judge   (c) honest
   (d) scene   (e) separate   (f) measure

6. List words are:
   (a) celebrate   (b) exercise   (c) author
   (d) future   (e) remember

7. judge, experience, remember, guess, increase, exercise, measure, centre, separate, celebrate, imagine

   Note: Words can be used in different ways.
   For example: **judge** can be a noun—the judge
   separate can be used as an adjective—separate accounts.

| judge | regular | experience | remember | guess | recent | increase | scene | neighbour | honest |
| exercise | measure | centre | separate | future | celebrate | imagine | author | favourite | government |

1. Write the words in alphabetical order.

_____ _____ _____ _____ _____

_____ _____ _____ _____ _____

_____ _____ _____ _____ _____

_____ _____ _____ _____ _____

2. (a) Write the seven words ending in short 'er' (∂) sound; e.g. rubb**er**

_____

(b) What are the different letter combinations representing the short 'er' (∂) sound?

_____

3. These words have more than one meaning. Write two different sentences for each.

(a) centre _____

_____

(b) exercise _____

_____

(c) regular _____

_____

(d) experience _____

_____

(e) judge _____

_____

4. Write the word that means:

(a) truthful _____ (b) writer _____ (c) current _____

(d) estimate _____ (e) location _____ (f) dream _____

5. Write the base word for each.

(a) futuristic _____ (b) judgemental _____ (c) dishonestly _____

(d) scenic _____ (e) inseparable _____ (f) measurement_____

6. Underline the list words in each question and answer it.

(a) Which day do you like to celebrate the most? _____

(b) What kind of exercise do you do on a regular basis? _____

(c) Name your favourite author and one of the books he/she has written. _____

(d) What kind of work would you like to do in the future? _____

(e) What is something you will always remember? _____

7. Write the list words that can be used as a verb.

_____

_____

TEACHER INFORMATION

The *plural* of a word indicates more than one person or thing.

Adding an **s** is the most common way to make most singular words **plural**.

- For words ending in **y**, with a vowel before the **y**, just add **s**; e.g. **boy—boys**.

- For words ending in **y**, with a consonant before the **y**, change the **y** to **i** and add **es**; e.g. **lady—ladies**. Note: Proper nouns do not change; add an **s** only; e.g. **Mr and Mrs Henry—The Henrys**.

- For words ending in **sh, ch, s** or **x**, add **es**; e.g. **dish—dishes, church—churches, box—boxes, dress—dresses**.

- For words ending in **f** or **fe**, change the **f** or **fe** to **v** and add **es**; e.g. **leaf—leaves**. Note: There are exceptions such as chief, belief, chef and cafe. (These words would sound strange with a **v** sound.)

- For some words ending in **o** add an **s**; e.g. **piano—pianos, avocado—avocados, radio—radios**.

  For others, add **es**; e.g. **hero—heroes, tomato—tomatoes, potato—potatoes, cargo—cargoes**. Note: Some words ending in **o** now have two acceptable plural forms; e.g. **mosquitoes—mosquitos, buffaloes—buffalos**.

- For words that are hyphenated, add **s** to the main noun; e.g. **sister-in-law—sisters-in-law**.

- Some words retain the same form; e.g. **sheep, aircraft, fish, deer**.

- Some words change completely; e.g. **tooth—teeth, mouse—mice, child—children, foot—feet**.

Answers

1. (a) arguments   (b) celebrations   (c) continents   (d) exercises
   (e) experiences   (f) favourites   (g) problems   (h) increases

2. (a) businesses   (b) guesses   (c) speeches   (d) stashes   (e) scratches
   (f) smashes   (g) sandwiches   (h) snatches   (i) rashes   (j) switches
   (k) batches   (l) addresses   (m) For words ending in **sh, ch, s** or **x**, add **es**.

3. (a) studies   (b) histories   (c) properties   (d) communities   (e) supplies
   (f) qualities   (g) boundaries   (h) countries   (i) enemies   (j) dictionaries
   (k) For words ending in **y** with a consonant before **y**, change the **y** to **i** and add **es**.

4. (a) pianos   (b) radios   (c) patios   (d) kangaroos   (e) Eskimos
   (f) Euros   (g) tomatoes   (h) potatoes   (i) heroes   (j) mosquitoes/s
   (k) echoes   (l) dominoes

5. (a) There are two neighbouring **properties** that are rented to different **businesses**.
   (b) I had three **guesses** about who the **authors** were.
   (c) We wrote the **addresses** on all the **envelopes** and sent the **invitations** to the ten **people**.
   (d) The principal always gives two **speeches** at all the school **assemblies**.
   (e) My favourite **experiences** are the **ones** that I have whenever there are **holidays**.

6. Examples include: thief—thieves, leaf—leaves, belief—beliefs, scarf—scarves, loaf—loaves, life—lives, cliff—cliffs, wife—wives, knife—knives, half—halves, shelf—shelves

7. Sentences will differ. The plural form of each word is:
   (a) zeros or zeroes, taxes   (b) memories, scenes   (c) clashes, communities
   (d) robberies, torches   (e) women, mice

Plurals

1. **Add the correct plural ending for each word.**

   (a) argument_____ (b) celebration_____ (c) continent_____ (d) exercise_____

   (e) experience_____ (f) favourite_____ (g) problem_____ (h) increase_____

2. **Add the correct plural ending for each word.**

   (a) business_____ (b) guess_____ (c) speech_____ (d) stash_____ (e) scratch_____

   (f) smash_____ (g) sandwich_____ (h) snatch_____ (i) rash_____ (j) switch_____

   (k) batch_____ (l) address_____ (m) Write a rule for making these words plural.

   _____

3. **Write these words as plurals.**

   (a) study _____ (b) history _____ (c) property _____

   (d) community _____ (e) supply _____ (f) quality _____

   (g) boundary _____ (h) country _____ (i) enemy _____

   (j) dictionary _____ (k) Write a rule for making these words plural.

   _____

4. **Add the correct plural ending for each word.**

   (a) piano_____ (b) radio_____ (c) patio_____ (d) kangaroo_____

   (e) Eskimo_____ (f) Euro_____ (g) tomato_____ (h) potato_____

   (i) hero_____ (j) mosquito_____ (k) echo_____ (l) domino_____

5. **Write these sentences to show the correct plurals.**

   (a) There are two neighbouring property that are rented to different business.

   _____

   (b) I had three guess about who the author were.

   _____

   (c) We wrote the address on all the envelope and sent the invitation to the ten person.

   _____

   (d) The principal always give two speech at all the school assembly.

   _____

   (e) My favourite experience are the one that I have whenever there are holiday.

   _____

6. **Write another five words that end in *f* or *fe*. Write the plural form of each word.**

   _____thief_____ _____thieves_____ _____ _____

   _____ _____ _____

7. **Write a sentence using the plural forms of the two words given.**

   (a) zero, tax _____

   (b) memory, scene _____

   (c) clash, community _____

   (d) robbery, torch _____

   (e) woman, mouse _____

TEACHER INFORMATION

The *base word* is the main part of the word; e.g. in**depend**ent.

Prefixes and suffixes are added to a base word to change its meaning.

These new words are called **derivatives**.

Answers

1. (a) guess   (b) recent   (c) argue
   (d) honest   (e) scribe   (f) scene
   (g) mean   (h) predict   (i) differ

2. (a) I will continue. I **continued**. I am **continuing**. It was **discontinued**. They are **discontinuing** it.
   (b) I had an experience. I had many **experiences**. I **experienced** it. I am **experiencing** it. She is **inexperienced**.
   (c) I will predict the weather. She **predicts** it. I am **predicting** it. I **predicted** it. It's very **predictable**. That was **unpredictable**.
   (d) I wrote a question. There were two **questions**. I **questioned** her. She is **questioning** me. It's very **questionable**.

3. Answers may include:
   (a) govern—governs, governed, governing, government, governments
   (b) value—values, valued, valuing, valuable, invaluable, valuables, devalues
   (c) condition—conditions, conditioned, conditioning, conditionally, unconditioned, unconditional
   (d) judge—judged, judges, judging, misjudge, judgement, judgements, misjudgment, misjudgments
   (e) image—images, imaging, imagination(s), imagine, imagined, imaginary, imaginative, imagery

4. (a) Both of my **parents** attended the teacher conference on Wednesday night.
   (b) My **grandparents** are retired now and enjoy spending time with their grandchildren.
   (c) It's your **parental** responsibility to ensure your children are at home after dark.

5. (a) After the survey was complete, we **graphed** the results to show the information clearly.
   (b) They took digital **photographs** of the class excursion and created a photo board to display.
   (c) I enjoy learning **geography** because I'm interested in distant places.

6. (a) Her business is based on **developing** fashionable, practical sleepwear for teenagers.
   (b) The new **development** will go ahead and the apartments will be available next year.
   (c) The tiny baby's lungs were **underdeveloped** because he was born premature.

7. Sentences will vary.

Base words

A *base word* is the main part of a word. Other words can be made from a base word by adding prefixes and suffixes. These new words are called *derivatives*.

1. **Write each base word.**

    (a) guessed ＿＿＿＿＿＿ (b) recently ＿＿＿＿＿＿ (c) argument ＿＿＿＿＿＿

    (d) honestly ＿＿＿＿＿＿ (e) describe ＿＿＿＿＿＿ (f) scenic ＿＿＿＿＿＿

    (g) meaning ＿＿＿＿＿＿ (h) prediction ＿＿＿＿＿＿ (i) difference ＿＿＿＿＿＿

2. **Write the base word to complete these.**

    (a) I will continue. I ＿＿＿＿＿ed. I am ＿＿＿＿＿ing. It was dis＿＿＿＿＿ed. They are dis＿＿＿＿＿ing it.

    (b) I had an experience. I had many ＿＿＿＿＿s. I ＿＿＿＿＿ed it. I am ＿＿＿＿＿ing it. She is in＿＿＿＿＿ed.

    (c) I will predict the weather. She ＿＿＿＿＿s it. I am ＿＿＿＿＿ing it. I ＿＿＿＿＿ed it. It's very ＿＿＿＿＿able. That was un＿＿＿＿＿able.

    (d) I wrote a question. There were two ＿＿＿＿＿s. I ＿＿＿＿＿ed her. She is ＿＿＿＿＿ing me. It's very ＿＿＿＿＿able.

3. **Write five new words (derivatives) for each base word.**

    (a) govern ＿＿＿＿ ＿＿＿＿ ＿＿＿＿ ＿＿＿＿ ＿＿＿＿

    (b) value ＿＿＿＿ ＿＿＿＿ ＿＿＿＿ ＿＿＿＿ ＿＿＿＿

    (c) condition ＿＿＿＿ ＿＿＿＿ ＿＿＿＿ ＿＿＿＿ ＿＿＿＿

    (d) judge ＿＿＿＿ ＿＿＿＿ ＿＿＿＿ ＿＿＿＿ ＿＿＿＿

    (e) image ＿＿＿＿ ＿＿＿＿ ＿＿＿＿ ＿＿＿＿ ＿＿＿＿

4. **Add to the base word *parent* to complete each sentence.**

    (a) Both of my ＿＿＿＿＿＿＿ attended the teacher conference on Wednesday night.

    (b) My ＿＿＿＿＿＿＿ are retired now and enjoy spending time with their grandchildren.

    (c) It's your ＿＿＿＿＿＿＿ responsibility to ensure your children are at home after dark.

5. **Add to the base word *graph* to complete each sentence.**

    (a) After the survey was complete, we ＿＿＿＿＿＿＿ the results to show the information clearly.

    (b) They took digital ＿＿＿＿＿＿＿ of the class excursion and created a photo board to display.

    (c) I enjoy learning ＿＿＿＿＿＿＿ because I'm interested in distant places.

6. **Add to the base word *develop* to complete each sentence.**

    (a) Her business is based on ＿＿＿＿＿＿＿ fashionable, practical sleepwear for teenagers.

    (b) The new ＿＿＿＿＿＿＿ will go ahead and the apartments will be available next year.

    (c) The tiny baby's lungs were ＿＿＿＿＿＿＿ because he was born premature.

7. **Write two sentences using words made by adding to the base word *popular*.**

    ＿＿＿＿＿＿＿＿＿＿＿＿＿＿＿＿＿＿＿＿＿＿＿＿＿＿＿＿＿＿＿

    ＿＿＿＿＿＿＿＿＿＿＿＿＿＿＿＿＿＿＿＿＿＿＿＿＿＿＿＿＿＿＿

TEACHER INFORMATION

A **prefix** is one or more letters added to the beginning of a base word to change its meaning; e.g. **dis**like, **un**happy, **re**play, **ir**responsible, **mis**understood, **im**proper, **dis**appear, **pre**heat, **il**legal.

Answers

1. (a) incomplete (b) immature (c) disobey
   (d) unsure (e) disadvantage (f) triangle
   (g) unavailable (h) discontinue (i) irregular
   (j) indifference (k) immobile (l) dissolve/resolve

2. Sentences will vary. Meaning should be clear; for example: heat *before*, pay *before*.

3. (a) submarine—vessel that can travel under water
   (b) substandard—below standard; inferior
   (c) subheading—smaller heading under main title
   (d) subeditor—assistant editor (who edits and corrects other people's work)
   (e) submerge—to put under water
   (f) subway—underground passage or tunnel

4. Sentences will vary. Meaning should be clear; for example: *wrongly* judge, *wrongly* watch

5. (a) anticlockwise—opposite to the normal rotation of hands on a clock
   (b) antisocial—opposed or unable to associate with others
   (c) antibacterial—treatment against germs
   (d) antidepressant—treatment against depression
   (e) antifreeze—liquid used to unfreeze
   (f) antiperspirant——treatment against perspiration; deodorant

Prefixes

A *prefix* is used at the beginning of a base word to change its meaning.

1. **Add a prefix to each of these words.**

(a) _____complete   (b) _____mature   (c) _____obey

(d) _____sure   (e) _____advantage   (f) _____angle

(g) _____available   (h) _____continue   (i) _____regular

(j) _____difference   (k) _____mobile   (l) _____solve

OBEY!

2. **The prefix *pre* means *before*. Use each word in a sentence to show meaning.**

(a) preheat _____

(b) prepay _____

(c) premixed _____

(d) preset _____

(e) preschool _____

(f) preview _____

3. **The prefix *sub* means *under*. Write a definition for each word.**

(a) submarine _____

(b) substandard _____

(c) subheading _____

(d) subeditor _____

(e) submerge _____

(f) subway _____

4. **The prefix *mis* means *wrongly*. Use each word in a sentence to show meaning.**

(a) misjudge _____

(b) mismatch _____

(c) misbehave _____

(d) misplace _____

(e) misprint _____

(f) mistrust _____

5. **The prefix *anti* means *opposed to* or *against*. Write a definition for each word.**

(a) anticlockwise _____

(b) antisocial _____

(c) antibacterial _____

(d) antidepressant _____

(e) antifreeze _____

(f) antiperspirant _____

TEACHER INFORMATION

A **suffix** is one or more letters added to the end of a base word to add to its meaning; e.g. care**less**, help**ful**, thin**ly**, walk**er**, agree**ment**, talk**ing**, break**able**, fam**ous**, neat**ness**, self**ish**.

Answers

1. (a) measurement　(b) separateness　(c) anxiousness　(d) argument
   (e) disappointment　(f) plumpness　(g) sturdiness　(h) government
   (i) nervousness　(j) judgement

2. Answers will vary and may include:
   (a) discover—s, ed, ing, y, ies
   (b) amaze—s, d, ing, ment
   (c) soft—ly, ness, er, est
   (d) mouth—s, ed, ing, ful(s)
   (e) journal—s, ist(s), ism
   (f) post—s, ed, ing, er, al, age
   (g) graph—s, ed, ing, ical, ic(s)
   (h) invent—s, ed, ing, or, ion, ive
   (i) object—s, ed, ing, or, ive(s)
   (j) impress—es, ed, ing, ive, ion(able)

3. (a) Sentences will vary. Meanings should be clear. For example:
   (i) creation—the act of creating, bringing into being, producing, causing to exist
   (ii) confusion—disorder, lack of clarity, bewilderment
   (iii) election—the selection of a person(s) for office by vote
   (iv) preparation—a proceeding, measure or provision by which one prepares for something
   (v) conclusion—the end or close, final part
   (vi) celebration—the act of observing a day or event with ceremonies
   (b) (i) condition　(ii) operation　(iii) promotion
   (iv) pension　(v) discussion　(vi) conclusion
   (vii) commotion　(viii) possession

4. Sentences will vary. Meanings should be clear. For example:
   (a) possible—that may or can be
   (b) sensible—showing good sense, judgement
   (c) terrible—dreadful, awful
   (d) visible—able to be seen
   (e) responsible—accountable, capable
   (f) edible—able to be eaten

5. Meanings should be clear. For example:
   (a) native—belonging by birth, occurring in nature
   (b) protective—the quality of defending
   (c) expensive—costly, not cheap
   (d) impressive—making a deep mark on mind or senses
   (e) distinctive—difference, individual
   (f) intensive—concentrated, emphasised

6. Answers will vary.

Suffixes

1. **Adding the suffixes –ment and –ness will change a word to a noun. Add the correct suffix to each word.**

   (a) measure_____ (b) separate_____ (c) anxious_____ (d) argue_____ (e) disappoint_____

   (f) plump_____ (g) sturdy_____ (h) govern_____ (i) nervous_____ (j) judge_____

2. **Add different suffixes to each of these words.**

   (a) discover_____ (b) amaze_____ (c) soft_____ (d) mouth_____ (e) journal_____

   (f) post_____ (g) graph_____ (h) invent_____ (i) object_____ (j) impress_____

3. **The suffix –ion means** *an action, state* **or** *quality*. **Using this suffix creates a noun.**

   (a) Use each word in a sentence to show its meaning.

      (i)   creation   _____

      (ii)   confusion   _____

      (iii) election   _____

      (iv)   preparation _____

      (v)   conclusion   _____

      (vi)   celebration _____

   (b) Circle the **sh** (as in *ship*) sound in these words.

      (i)   condition   (ii) operation   (iii) promotion   (iv) pension

      (v)   discussion   (vi) conclusion   (vii) commotion   (viii) possession

4. **The suffix –ible means** *capable of being*. **Adding this suffix creates an adjective. Use each word in a sentence to show its meaning.**

   (a) possible   _____

   (b) sensible   _____

   (c) terrible   _____

   (d) visible   _____

   (e) responsible   _____

   (f) edible   _____

5. **The suffix –ive means** *connected with* **or** *like*. **Adding this suffix creates an adjective. Write a definition for each word.**

   (a) native   _____

   (b) protective   _____

   (c) expensive   _____

   (d) impressive   _____

   (e) distinctive   _____

   (f) intensive   _____

6. **Write two words for each suffix.**

   (a) -ly   _____ _____   (b) -ful   _____ _____

   (c) -er   _____ _____   (d) -less _____ _____

   (e) -ing _____ _____   (f) -or   _____ _____

   (g) -ist _____ _____   (h) -ous   _____ _____

Answers

1. Numbering starts from top to bottom.
   (a) amount, cheap, famous, notice, public, visitor .... (4, 3, 1, 6, 5, 2)
   (b) believe, calm, either, heavy, useful, weight................................. (2, 5, 3, 1, 6, 4)
   (c) chief, dangerous, except, handle, manage, thief .... (2, 6, 4, 3, 1, 5)
   (d) beginning, cruel, excuse, message, reason, though .... (3, 1, 6, 2, 5, 4)
   (e) address, discover, important, promise, sign, through................. (5, 1, 4, 6, 2, 3)

2. Numbering starts from top to bottom.
   (a) accident, afford, although, anxious, argue, author .... (5, 3, 4, 1, 2, 6)
   (b) careful, centre, cheap, condition, cruel, current......................... (3, 4, 2, 1, 6, 5)
   (c) dangerous, decide, disappoint, download, dragon, dusty .... (3, 2, 1, 4, 6, 5)
   (d) separate, sign, solve, special, straight, subtraction .... (5, 4, 1, 2, 6, 3)

3. (a) reason, recent, regular, reply, rescue
   (b) behind, believe, beneath, berry, beyond
   (c) fibres, fifty, figure, finally, firstly
   (d) pacific, palace, pamper, pancake, partner

4. Numbering starts from top to bottom.
   (a) disappoint, discover, disease, disgrace, dismay, distract............ (3, 2, 1, 4, 6, 5)
   (b) problem, professional, programme, project, promote, property. (4, 1, 6, 5, 2, 3)
   (c) combat, comedian, comfortable, common, complain, comrade. (4, 5, 3, 1, 6, 2)
   (d) uniform, uninvited, union, unique, unison, united......................... (6, 1, 3, 4, 5, 2)

5. complain, complete, completion, complex, complexion, complicate, complication, compliment

6. Answers will vary.

7. Answers will vary.

Alphabetical order

1. Number the boxes to show the alphabetical order of each list.

(a) notice   (b) calm   (c) dangerous   (d) excuse   (e) sign

    famous   useful   thief   beginning   address

    amount   either   handle   though   promise

    visitor   believe   except   cruel   through

    public   weight   chief   reason   discover

    cheap   heavy   manage   message   important

2. These words all start with the same letter. Show the correct alphabetical order.

(a) argue   (b) cheap   (c) disappoint   (d) straight

    although   condition   decide   special

    anxious   centre   dangerous   separate

    accident   careful   download   sign

    afford   current   dusty   subtraction

    author   cruel   dragon   solve

3. These words all start with the same two letters. Write each list in alphabetical order.

(a) rescue, regular, recent, reply, reason   _____

(b) believe, beyond, behind, beneath, berry   _____

(c) figure, fibres, finally, firstly, fifty   _____

(d) palace, partner, pacific, pancake, pamper   _____

4. These words all start with the same three letters. Show the correct alphabetical order.

(a) disease   (b) project   (c) common   (d) united

    discover   problem   complain   uniform

    disappoint   property   comfortable   union

    disgrace   promote   combat   unique

    distract   professional   comrade   unison

    dismay   programme   comedian   uninvited

5. Write these words in alphabetical order.

compliment   *complexion*   *complicate*   *complete*   *complain*   *complex*   *completion*   *complication*

_____ _____ _____ _____

_____ _____ _____ _____

6. Write the first names of five favourite people in alphabetical order.

_____ _____ _____ _____ _____

7. Write the names of five favourite foods in alphabetical order.

_____ _____ _____ _____ _____

PUPIL NAME

TEACHER INFORMATION

A **syllable** is a unit of sound which contains one vowel sound. All words are made up of one or more syllables.

Prefixes and suffixes are usually separate syllables; e.g. **im/prove/ment**.

Compound words have two or more syllables; e.g. **note/book, out/side, sun/shine**.

When a word has double consonants, separate syllables between these letters; e.g. **yel/low, scrib/ble, gram/mar**.

Words ending in **-tle, -ble, -dle, -ple, -gle, -cle, -fle** and **-zle** are usually separate syllables; e.g. **whis/tle, sta/ble, han/dle, sam/ple, jin/gle, trea/cle, ri/fle, puz/zle**.

Base words with a vowel–consonant–vowel pattern usually divide before the consonant; e.g. **po/lice, do/nor, o/pen, de/lete, a/gent, si/lent**.

Base words with a vowel–consonant–vowel–consonant pattern usually divide between the consonants; e.g. **doc/tor, pic/ture, cen/sus, con/cert**.

Answers

1. (a) hon/est   (b) re/cent   (c) cen/tre   (d) fu/ture
    (e) ar/gue   (f) mea/sure   (g) cre/ate   (h) ex/act
    (i) stud/y   (j) gov/ern

2. (a) part/ner/ship   (b) re/mem/ber   (c) sep/ar/ate   (d) i/ma/gine
    (e) ex/er/cise   (f) reg/u/lar   (g) cel/e/brate   (h) gov/ern/ment
    (i) qual/i/ty   (j) prop/er/ty

3. (a) al/though   (b) mis/take   (c) graph/ing   (d) soft/ly
    (e) pre/pay   (f) sub/way   (g) un/sure   (h) judge/ment
    (i) mis/guide   (j) bi/plane   (k) pre/view   (l) im/prove

4. (a) guess/work   (b) down/load   (c) chop/stick   (d) brief/case
    (e) feed/back   (f) guide/line   (g) proof/read   (h) search/light
    (i) worth/while   (j) tooth/paste   (k) waist/line   (l) broad/band

5. (a) sur/round   (b) lug/gage   (c) af/ford   (d) driz/zle
    (e) gram/mar   (f) ad/dress   (g) sud/den   (h) dol/lar
    (i) pil/low   (j) scan/ner   (k) daz/zle   (l) yel/low

6. (a) a fiction book—novel   (b) a sketch or plan—design
    (c) make—create   (d) a kind of phone—mobile
    (e) times two—double   (f) a diary—journal
    (g) rectangular shape—oblong   (h) not remember—forget
    (i) quiet—silent

7. (a) 26 letters—alphabet   (b) group of sentences—paragraph
    (c) not the same—different   (d) a guess or future forecast—prediction
    (e) well-liked—popular   (f) a glossy booklet—magazine
    (g) physical activity—exercise   (h) non-driving traveller—passenger

8. One syllable—sweep, rough, doubt, scene
    Two syllables—increase, afford, argue, litre, recent
    Three syllables—favourite, condition, accident, division, uselessly
    Four syllables—community, immediate, participate, calculator, entertainment

Syllables

A *syllable* is a word or part of a word. There is a vowel *sound* in every syllable.

1. **Circle the two syllables in each of these words; e.g. ex/treme.**

   (a) honest   (b) recent   (c) centre   (d) future   (e) argue

   (f) measure   (g) create   (h) exact   (i) study   (j) govern

2. **Circle the three syllables in each of these words; e.g. eas/i/er.**

   (a) partnership   (b) remember   (c) separate   (d) imagine   (e) exercise

   (f) regular   (g) celebrate   (h) government   (i) quality   (j) property

3. **Prefixes and suffixes are separate syllables. Show the syllables in these words; e.g. re/source.**

   (a) although   (b) mistake   (c) graphing   (d) softly

   (e) prepay   (f) subway   (g) unsure   (h) judgement

   (i) misguide   (j) biplane   (k) preview   (l) improve

4. **Compound words are separate syllables. Show the syllables in these words.; e.g. side/track.**

   (a) guesswork   (b) download   (c) chopstick   (d) briefcase

   (e) feedback   (f) guideline   (g) proofread   (h) searchlight

   (i) worthwhile   (j) toothpaste   (k) waistline   (l) broadband

5. **When a word has double consonants, separate syllables between these letters. Show the syllables in these words.**

   (a) surround   (b) luggage   (c) afford   (d) drizzle

   (e) grammar   (f) address   (g) sudden   (h) dollar

   (i) pillow   (j) scanner   (k) dazzle   (l) yellow

6. **Write a two-syllable word for each. The first syllable is provided.**

   (a) a fiction book   nov_____   (b) a sketch or plan   de_____   (c) make   cre_____

   (d) a kind of phone   mo_____   (e) times two   dou_____   (f) a diary   journ_____

   (g) rectangular shape   ob_____   (h) not remember   for_____   (i) quiet   si_____

7. **Write a three-syllable word for each. The first syllable is provided.**

   (a) 26 letters   al_____   (b) group of sentences   par_____

   (c) not the same   dif_____   (d) a guess or future forecast   pre_____

   (e) well-liked   pop_____   (f) a glossy booklet   mag_____

   (g) physical activity   ex_____   (h) non-driving traveller   pas_____

8. **Put the words into groups of one, two, three and four syllables.**

   increase   sweep   community   afford   argue   immediate   favourite   condition   participate
   rough   accident   litre   division   calculator   doubt   uselessly   recent   scene   entertainment

One syllable	Two syllables	Three syllables	Four syllables

TEACHER INFORMATION

Synonyms are words that are similar in meaning. Synonyms allow descriptions to be more precise and can avoid monotony. Although a group of words may be synonyms, there are usually slight differences in meaning; e.g. synonyms for **walk** include: **saunter, stroll, amble, pace, go, move, hike** and **stride**.

Answers

1. (a) verse   (b) collect   (c) nation
   (d) payment   (e) weary   (f) biscuit
   (g) dawn   (h) complain   (i) breeze
   (j) finale   (k) refuse   (l) junior

2. (a) choose   (b) calm   (c) ordinary
   (d) answer   (e) overlook   (f) mischief

3. (a) demolish   (b) fractured   (c) covered
   (d) graceful   (e) leave

4. Answers may include:
   (a) centre   (b) imagine   (c) rescue
   (d) author   (e) argue   (f) enough

5. Answers may include:
   (a) I wrote in my **diary** and **drew/made** a **picture/drawing** on the same page.
   (b) I only ate a **part** of what Mum **cooked** because I felt **ill/sick**.
   (c) The **journey** was **tiring** because we **drove** so far without a **rest/stop**.
   (d) We had to **answer** five maths **problems** at the **start** of the **lesson**.
   (e) The **land/house** my parents **own** is a regular size with a **large** outdoor area.
   (f) Cassie was **well-liked** by other children and **studied** hard to **get/obtain** **excellent/great** marks.

Synonyms

Synonyms are words that have the same or similar meaning.

1. Choose a synonym from the list to match each word.

(a) poem _____   (b) gather _____

(c) country _____   (d) fee _____

(e) tired _____   (f) cookie _____

(g) sunrise _____   (h) whinge _____

(i) wind _____   (j) ending _____

(k) deny _____   (l) young _____

weary	nation
biscuit	breeze
finale	collect
verse	complain
dawn	refuse
junior	payment

2. Circle the word in each list that is not a synonym.

(a) choice	(b) anxious	(c) special	(d) problem	(e) remember	(f) accident
pick	calm	unique	puzzle	memorise	mischief
option	nervous	unusual	answer	recall	mishap
choose	worried	exclusive	challenge	reminisce	mistake
selection	uneasy	ordinary	obstacle	overlook	misfortune
preference	restless	exceptional	difficulty	recollect	collision

3. Select the better of the two synonyms in each sentence.

(a) The council decided to [demolish | destroy] the old building.

(b) The x-rays showed he had [fractured | cracked] his arm.

(c) The houses were [hidden | covered] in snow during the storm.

(d) The dancer's moves were extremely [beautiful | graceful].

(e) The express train will [escape | leave] from the station at 8 am.

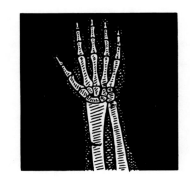

4. Write a synonym for each word.

(a) middle _____   (b) dream _____   (c) save _____

(d) writer _____   (e) fight _____   (f) sufficient _____

5. Write synonyms above the underlined words.

(a) I wrote in my <u>journal</u> and <u>created</u> an <u>illustration</u> on the same page.

(b) I only ate a <u>fraction</u> of what Mum <u>made</u> because I felt <u>unwell</u>.

(c) The <u>trip</u> was <u>exhausting</u> because we <u>travelled</u> so far without a <u>break</u>.

(d) We had to <u>solve</u> five maths <u>equations</u> at the <u>beginning</u> of the <u>session</u>.

(e) The <u>property</u> my parents <u>have</u> is a regular size with a <u>big</u> outdoor area.

(f) Cassie was <u>admired</u> by other <u>children</u> and <u>worked</u> hard to <u>receive</u> <u>high</u> marks.

TEACHER INFORMATION

Antonyms are words that are opposite in meaning. Antonyms can add a contrast in description or feeling. Many words take a prefix to create an antonym; e.g. **happy—unhappy**.

Answers

1. (a) anxious   (b) argue   (c) disappoint
   (d) future   (e) separate   (f) honest
   (g) increase   (h) problem   (i) regular
   (j) remember   (k) double   (l) fraction

2. Answers may include:
   (a) sweet   (b) senior   (c) covered
   (d) child   (e) ancient   (f) few
   (g) poor   (h) rude
   (i) extraordinary/exceptional

3. (a) rare   (b) end   (c) exposed
   (d) peaceful   (e) gradual   (f) worthless

4. Answers may include:
   (a) The film was so **exciting** and I was **happy** that **he** had chosen it.
   (b) Matilda had the **most** amount of food but she was the **oldest** and **biggest**.
   (c) **She** took the **clean** rags **in** and put them **above** the bench.
   (d) The cars were **slowing** as they went **up** the **crooked** road and **under** the bridge.
   (e) The **new** tree was **tiny** and when we walked **behind** it we could see the birds near the **bottom**.
   (f) **Her** bedroom was **dirty** and **untidy** and **her** wardrobe was **empty**.

5. (a) bravely—cowardly   (b) heated—cooled
   (c) nephew—niece   (d) careful—careless
   (e) complain—praise   (f) queen—king

Antonyms

Antonyms **are words that are opposite in meaning.**

1. Choose an antonym from the list to match each word.

future	increase	fraction	remember	argue	separate
double	anxious	problem	disappoint	honest	regular

(a) calm _____

(b) agree _____

(c) please _____

(d) past _____

(e) together _____

(f) dishonest _____

(g) decrease _____

(h) solution _____

(i) irregular _____

(j) forget _____

(k) single _____

(l) whole _____

2. Write an antonym for each word.

(a) sour _____

(b) junior _____

(c) bare _____

(d) adult _____

(e) modern _____

(f) several _____

(g) wealthy _____

(h) polite _____

(i) ordinary _____

3. Write the antonym from each list.

(a) common   ordinary   normal   rare   everyday   _____

(b) end   beginning   start   onset   commencement   _____

(c) safe   secure   protected   locked   exposed   _____

(d) angry   peaceful   irate   annoyed   cross   furious   _____

(e) immediate   direct   pressing   gradual   instant   urgent   _____

(f) valuable   precious   priceless   worthless   expensive   important   _____

4. Write antonyms above the underlined words.

(a) The film was so <u>boring</u> and I was <u>unhappy</u> that <u>she</u> had chosen it.

(b) Matilda had the <u>least</u> amount of food but she was the <u>youngest</u> and <u>smallest</u>.

(c) <u>He</u> took the <u>dirty</u> rags <u>out</u> and put them <u>below</u> the bench.

(d) The cars were <u>speeding</u> as they went <u>down</u> the <u>straight</u> road and <u>over</u> the bridge.

(e) The <u>old</u> tree was <u>gigantic</u> and when we walked <u>in front of</u> it we could see the birds near the <u>top</u>.

(f) <u>His</u> bedroom was <u>clean</u> and <u>neat</u> and <u>his</u> wardrobe was <u>full</u>.

5. Write the two antonyms from each list.

(a) bravely   cowardly   publicly   carefully   cleverly   _____ _____

(b) heated   warm   tasty   cooled   iced   _____ _____

(c) aunt   grandma   nephew   cousin   niece   _____ _____

(d) careful   careless   uncaring   cared   caretaker   _____ _____

(e) complain   comfort   comfortable   prepare   praise   _____ _____

(f) queen   king   princess   palace   dump   _____ _____

TEACHER INFORMATION

Homophones are words that sound the same but have different meanings; e.g. **cereal – serial, know – no, feat – feet, stare – stair**.

Homographs are words that are spelt the same but have different meanings and may or may not sound the same.

Examples:

- **bow** (rhymes with cow)—a verb meaning to bend the body as a sign of respect
- **bow** (rhymes with low)—a noun meaning a looped knot
- **fair**—a noun meaning a group of sideshows
- **fair**—an adjective meaning not cloudy.

Answers

1. (a) homophones — nun, none
   (b) homophones — aloud, allowed
   (c) homographs — bow, bow
   (d) homographs — lead, lead
   (e) homophones — miner, minor
   (f) homographs — bill, bill
   (g) homophones — seen, scene
   (h) homographs — row, row

2. (a) wait
   (b) choose
   (c) waist
   (d) sole
   (e) haul
   (f) sight
   (g) bored
   (h) hair
   (i) weigh
   (j) break
   (k) piece
   (l) through

3. These words are **homophones**. Sentences will vary.
   Examples:
   (a) She **passed** the exam.
   (b) He walked **past** her.
   (c) The electric **current** was disconnected.
   (d) The dried grape was a **currant**.
   (e) She was **poor** because she had no money.
   (f) The tiny skin opening is a **pore**.
   (g) **Pour** the water.
   (h) The dog's **paw** was injured.

4. These words are **homographs**. Sentences will vary.
   Examples:
   (a) She has **fair** skin.
   (b) We went to the **fair**.
   (c) Dad was **cross**.
   (d) A **cross** marked the spot.
   (e) The teachers **mark** our exams.
   (f) The glass left a **mark** on the table.

Homophones and homographs

Homophones are words that sound the same but have different meanings; e.g. *fare* and *fair*.

Homographs are words that are spelt the same, have different meanings and may or may not sound the same; e.g. *swallow*, *wind* (rhymes with *kind*) and *wind* (rhymes with *tinned*).

1. **Write whether these pairs of sentences contain homophones or homographs.**

   (a) The nun worked in the church garden. She wanted to plant herbs but she had none. _____

   (b) Christy was speaking aloud. She wasn't really allowed to do that in class. _____

   (c) She had a blue bow in her hair. He was sure to bow correctly when he met the Queen. _____

   (d) There was a lead pipe outside the house. It lead to a large drain. _____

   (e) The miner was finishing his shift. He found a minor bruise on his leg. _____

   (f) I decided to pay the bill online. There was a duck near the window with a worm in its bill. _____

   (g) I hadn't seen the play before. My friend said there was a scene where I might cry. _____

   (h) The people were supposed to sit in a row. Two men had a row and one sat at the back. _____

2. **Write a homophone for each word.**

   (a) weight _____   (b) chews _____   (c) waste _____

   (d) soul _____   (e) hall _____   (f) site _____

   (g) board _____   (h) hare _____   (i) way _____

   (j) brake _____   (k) peace _____   (l) threw _____

3. **Write sentences to show the meaning of each word. These words are h_____.**

   (a) passed _____

   (b) past _____

   (c) current _____

   (d) currant _____

   (e) poor _____

   (f) pore _____

   (g) pour _____

   (h) paw _____

4. **Write two sentences to show different meanings for each word. These words are _____.**

   (a) fair _____

   (b) fair _____

   (c) cross _____

   (d) cross _____

   (e) mark _____

   (f) mark _____

PUPIL NAME

TEACHER INFORMATION

A **compound word** is formed by joining two or more words.

Examples include:

- waterfall, desktop, notebook, driveway, football, daybreak, nightfall, downcast, halfway, footloose, fireproof, hard-wearing, long-sighted, three-quarters, do-it-yourself.

Answers

1. Answers may include:
   - (a) carport, porthole
   - (b) outside, dropout
   - (c) workman, overwork
   - (d) understand, hereunder
   - (e) screenplay, smokescreen
   - (f) breakfast, daybreak
   - (g) overact, walkover
   - (h) plaything, overplay
   - (i) cupcake, teacup
   - (j) handbook, underhand
   - (k) fireman, backfire
   - (l) pathway, footpath

2. Answers may include:
   - (a) foot—ball, stool, fall, bridge, lights, loose, man, note, path, print, rest
   - (b) house—hold, work, wife, boat, flies, keeper, coat
   - (c) main—land, stream, stay, sail, mast, spring, line, sheet
   - (d) side—ways, board, walk, kick, car, long, swipe, line, step, stroke
   - (e) short—hand, coming, stop, fall, age, bread, cake

3. (a) copycat
   (b) nightmare
   (c) withdraw
   (d) timetable
   (e) schoolteacher
   (f) passport
   (g) runway
   (h) checkmate

4. Answers will vary.

5. Answers will vary.

Compound words

1. **Use each word to make two compound words; e.g.** *day—daylight, today*.

   (a) port _____ (b) out _____

   (c) work _____ (d) under _____

   (e) screen _____ (f) break _____

   (g) over _____ (h) play _____

   (i) cup _____ (j) hand _____

   (k) fire _____ (l) path _____

2. **Write six words that can be added to make compound words.**

   (a) foot _____

   (b) house _____

   (c) main _____

   (d) side _____

   (e) short _____

3. **Use the clue to write a compound word.**

   (a) A person who imitates someone else. _c_ _____ _c_ _____

   (b) A frightening dream. _n_ _____

   (c) Something you do when taking money out of an account. _w_ _____

   (d) A schedule of events. _t_ _____

   (e) A person who educates others in a place of learning. _s_ _____

   (f) A document used as identification when travelling. _p_ _____

   (g) A measured strip of land used by aircraft. _r_ _____

   (h) The winning position in a game of chess. _c_ _____

4. **Write your own clue for each compound word. Don't use any part of the word in your clue.**

   (a) armchair _____

   (b) driveway _____

   (c) hairdresser _____

   (d) flashlight _____

   (e) storeroom _____

   (f) popcorn _____

   (g) masterpiece _____

   (h) waterfall _____

5. **Use each pair of compound words in a sentence.**

   (a) drumstick, daytime _____

   (b) roundabout, carport _____

   (c) cupcake, somebody _____

   (d) earring, haircut _____

   (e) waistline, sometimes _____

TEACHER INFORMATION

An ***abbreviation*** is a word written in a shortened form. Generally, a full stop is used to show that part of the word is missing:

- population—pop.   tablespoon—tbsp.

No full stop is used when the first and last letters are used;

- Doctor—Dr   Road—Rd

Abbreviations which consist of more than one capital letter do not generally require full stops;

- DOB (date of birth)   PO (post office)

Answers

1. (a) can't   (b) they're   (c) it's   (d) I've   (e) doesn't   (f) we'll
   (g) I'd   (h) that's   (i) aren't   (j) she'd   (k) wasn't   (l) it'll

2. (a) **I'm** staying with my cousins and **we're** going somewhere I **haven't** been before.
   (b) **She's** having a special day that **we've** all decided **we'll** attend.
   (c) **It's** a condition that **can't** be easily treated, so **you'll** have to be careful.
   (d) We **shouldn't** accept his story because **he's** not being honest or **doesn't** know the truth.
   (e) **They've** been to the beach and **they're** deciding about where **they'll** eat lunch.
   (f) **That's** a great place and **I'm** glad **you're** going because **it'll** be fun.

3. (a) can't   I'll   they'll   (b) couldn't   they're   she'll   (c) That's   we've   don't   I'll
   (d) I'd   he's   don't   I've   (e) They've   that's   I'd   they've

4. (a) litre   (b) millilitre   (c) millimetre   (d) centimetre   (e) metre
   (f) kilometre   (g) kilogram   (h) gram   (i) second   (j) minute/minimum
   (k) hour   (l) year

5. (a) km/h   (b) temp.   (c) C   (d) max.   (e) min.   (f) approx.
   (g) e.g.   (h) esp.   (i) bet.   (j) govt   (k) MP

6. Answers will vary.

Abbreviated words

1. **Write the contractions for each.**

   (a) can not _____ (b) they are _____ (c) it is _____ (d) I have _____

   (e) does not _____ (f) we will _____ (g) I would _____ (h) that is _____

   (i) are not _____ (j) she would _____ (k) was not _____ (l) it will _____

2. **Write each sentence using the correct contractions.**

   (a) I am staying with my cousins and we are going somewhere I have not been before.

   _____

   (b) She is having a special day that we have all decided we will attend.

   _____

   (c) It is a condition that can not be easily treated, so you will have to be careful.

   _____

   (d) We should not accept his story because he is not being honest or does not know the truth.

   _____

   (e) They have been to the beach and they are deciding about where they will eat lunch.

   _____

   (f) That is a great place and I am glad you are going because it will be fun.

   _____

3. **Show where the apostrophe should be in each contraction.**

   (a) I cant afford to celebrate so Ill see if theyll come over for a barbecue.

   (b) She couldnt go to her regular appointment so theyre taking her out so shell have something to do.

   (c) Thats got to be the hardest work weve done and I dont think Ill be happy with the results.

   (d) Id much rather go home if hes not well so I dont get sick. Ive got a lot to do tomorrow.

   (e) Theyve got a great garden thats full of flowers and Id love to just sit and enjoy all theyve done.

4. **Write the word for each of these measurement abbreviations.**

   (a) L _____ (b) mL _____ (c) mm _____

   (d) cm _____ (e) m _____ (f) km _____

   (g) kg _____ (h) g _____ (i) sec. _____

   (j) min. _____ (k) hr _____ (l) yr _____

5. **Write the abbreviation for each of the following.**

   (a) kilometres per hour_____ (b) temperature _____ (c) Celsius _____ (d) maximum _____

   (e) minimum _____ (f) approximately_____ (g) example _____ (h) especially _____

   (i) between _____ (j) government _____ (k) Member of Parliament _____

6. (a) Use abbreviated words to write a text message you might send to a friend about your weekend plans.

   _____

   (b) Write the message in full.

   _____

TEACHER INFORMATION

Consonants which form digraphs (i.e. two letters making one sound) with other consonants include:

- **b**—after **m**; e.g. bo**mb**, thu**mb**
- **g**—before **n**; e.g. si**gn**, **gn**ome, and with **h**; e.g. **gh**ost
- **k**—before **n**; e.g. **kn**ee, **kn**ife
- **l**—e.g. ca**lm**, ta**lk**
- **n**—after **m**; e.g. hy**mn**, autu**mn**
- **p**—before **n**, **s** and **t**; e.g. **pn**eumonia, **ps**ychology, **pt**erodactyl
- **t**—after **s**; e.g. ca**st**le, li**st**en, ru**st**le
- **w**—before **r**; e.g. **wr**ite, **wr**ing, and before **h**; e.g. **wh**ole

Some consonants are silent when in a digraph with a vowel; e.g. i**s**land, **h**onest.

Answers

1. (a) honest—h   (b) heir—h   (c) plumber—b
   (d) salmon—l   (e) sword—w   (f) whether—h

2. (a) salmon   (b) plumber   (c) whether
   (d) sword   (e) honest   (f) heir

3. (a) co**mm**unity   (b) a**pp**ly   (c) disa**pp**oint
   (d) disa**pp**ear   (e) o**cc**asion   (f) reco**mm**end
   (g) shu**dd**er/shu**tt**er   (h) stu**tt**er   (i) o**pp**osite
   (j) o**pp**ortunity   (k) a**cc**o**mm**odation   (l) emba**rrass**

4. (a) kidnapped   (b) fatten   (c) worshipped
   (d) madden   (e) tunnelled   (f) rebelled
   Sentences will vary.

5. Answers may vary.
   (a) The Prime Minister hosted an **official** meeting with world leaders.
   (b) During the winter months it's nice to wear **flannel** pyjamas because they are warmer.
   (c) The **traffic** on the motorway was so bad that we were late for school.
   (d) If you equally divide a square in any direction it always has perfect **symmetry**.
   (e) When you want to send a file from your documents, **attach** it to your email.
   (f) I played goal shooter in the netball final and my **opponent** was much taller than me.

6. (a) At playschool we said a nursery **rhyme** every morning.
   (b) While we were watching a scary film, there was a loud **knock** at the door.
   (c) When we went into the event, we were given a coloured **wrist** band to prove we had paid.
   (d) The footballer was unable to complete the game because of a **knee** injury.
   (e) A beautiful **wreath** of colourful flowers was laid on top of the coffin.
   (f) The explorers finally found the **wreck** a long way under the water's surface.

7. (a) go**ss**ip   (b) hurricane   (c) ha**mm**er
   (d) su**ff**ocate   (e) bo**mb**   (f) hi**pp**opotamus
   (g) horrible   (h) **kn**ee
   Clues will vary.

Double and silent consonants

1. **Write the silent consonant in each word.**

   (a) honest _____ (b) heir _____ (c) plumber _____

   (d) salmon _____ (e) sword _____ (f) whether _____

2. **Match a word from Question 1 to each meaning.**

   (a) a type of fish _____ (b) a repair person _____

   (c) a homophone for weather _____ (d) a weapon with a long blade _____

   (e) truthful _____ (f) a homophone for *air* _____

3. **Write the missing double letters in each word.**

   (a) co_____unity (b) a_____ly (c) disa_____oint (d) disa_____ear (e) o_____asion

   (f) reco_____end (g) shu_____er (h) stu_____er (i) o_____osite (j) o_____ortunity

   (k) a_____o_____odation (l) emba_____a_____

4. **Write a new word by adding *ed* or *en*. Use the word in a sentence to show the new meaning.**

   (a) kidnap _____ _____

   (b) fat _____ _____

   (c) worship _____ _____

   (d) mad _____ _____

   (e) tunnel _____ _____

   (f) rebel _____ _____

5. **Complete each sentence with a double-lettered word.**

   (a) The Prime Minister hosted an _____ meeting with world leaders.

   (b) During the winter months it's nice to wear _____ pyjamas because they are warmer.

   (c) The _____ on the motorway was so bad that we were late for school.

   (d) If you equally divide a square in any direction it always has perfect _____.

   (e) When you want to send a file from your documents, _____ it to your email.

   (f) I played goal shooter in the netball final and my _____ was much taller than me.

6. **Complete each sentence with a word beginning with two consonants making one sound.**

   (a) At playschool we said a nursery _____ every morning.

   (b) While we were watching a scary film, there was a loud _____ at the door.

   (c) When we went into the event, we were given a coloured _____ band to prove we had paid.

   (d) The footballer was unable to complete the game because of a _____ injury.

   (e) A beautiful _____ of colourful flowers was laid on top of the coffin.

   (f) The explorers finally found the _____ a long way under the water's surface.

7. **Underline the double or silent consonants and write your own clue to match each word.**

   (a) gossip _____ (b) hurricane _____

   (c) hammer _____ (d) suffocate _____

   (e) bomb _____ (f) hippopotamus _____

   (g) horrible _____ (h) knee _____

Answers

1. (a) arguing   (b) celebrating   (c) centring
   (d) exercising   (e) experiencing   (f) imagining
   (g) measuring   (h) rescuing   (i) separating

2. (a) (i) passenger   (ii) surround   (iii) immediate
       (iv) business   (v) disappoint   (vi) afford
   (b) (i) favourite   (ii) scene   (iii) valuable
       (iv) continue   (v) luggage   (vi) practise
   (c) (i) celebration   (ii) condition   (iii) position
       (iv) imagination   (v) creation   (vi) prediction
   (d) (i) accidents   (ii) governments   (iii) disappoints
       (iv) affords   (v) authors   (vi) graphs
   (e) (i) neighbourly   (ii) recently   (iii) exactly
       (iv) meanly   (v) anxiously   (vi) honestly
   (f) (i) decide   (ii) notice   (iii) balance
       (iv) except   (v) difference   (vi) exercise

3. (a) neighbours   (b) histories   (c) women
   (d) surrounds   (e) properties   (f) qualities
   (g) novels   (h) sheep   (i) communities

4. (a) The **girls** were **especially** nice to the **new** teacher who was very **experienced**.
   (b) I had to **reduce** the size of one of the **graphs** I drew so they were **both equal** in height.
   (c) All **passengers** received **immediate decreases** in the **amounts** they **paid** for **their tickets**.
   (d) The two **businessmen** were **disappointed** when they didn't **receive** an **honest answer**.
   (e) **There** was a **separate discussion** by **one** side of the **government** over the **important** issue.

5. piece brief viewer achieving niece convenient

Identifying correct spelling

1. **These words are spelt incorrectly. Write them correctly.**

   (a) argueing _____ (b) celebrateing _____ (c) centreing _____

   (d) exerciseing _____ (e) experienceing _____ (f) imagineing _____

   (g) measureing _____ (h) rescueing _____ (i) separateing _____

2. **Each group of words has a similar error. Write each word correctly.**

   (a) (i) pasenger _____ (ii) suround _____ (iii) imediate _____

       (iv) busines _____ (v) disapoint _____ (vi) aford _____

   (b) (i) favourit _____ (ii) scen _____ (iii) valuabl _____

       (iv) continu _____ (v) luggag _____ (vi) practis _____

   (c) (i) celebrasion _____ (ii) condision _____ (iii) posision _____

       (iv) imaginasion _____ (v) creasion _____ (vi) predicsion _____

   (d) (i) accidentes _____ (ii) governmentes _____ (iii) disappointes _____

       (iv) affordes _____ (v) authores _____ (vi) graphes _____

   (e) (i) neighbourlly _____ (ii) recentlly _____ (iii) exactlly _____

       (iv) meanlly _____ (v) anxiouslly _____ (vi) honestlly _____

   (f) (i) deside _____ (ii) notise _____ (iii) balanse _____

       (iv) exsept _____ (v) differense _____ (vi) exersise _____

3. **These plural words are incorrect. Write each correctly.**

   (a) neighboures _____ (b) historys _____ (c) womans _____

   (d) surroundes _____ (e) propertyies _____ (f) qualityes _____

   (g) noveles _____ (h) sheeps _____ (i) communitys _____

4. **Underline the words spelt incorrectly. Write each sentence correctly.**

   (a) The girles were espesially nice to the knew teacher who was very expereinced.

   _____

   (b) I had to reduse the size of one of the graphes I drew so they were bothe equel in height.

   _____

   (c) All passenger received imediate decreeses in the amountes they payed for there tikets.

   _____

   (d) The two businessmans were disapointed when they didn't recieve an onest anser.

   _____

   (e) Their was a seperate discusion by won side of the goverment over the important issue.

   _____

5. **Rewrite only the words that are spelt incorrectly.**

neighbour	peice	either	breif	veiwer	acheiving	friendly	received	neice	conveneint

   _____

   _____

TEACHER INFORMATION

This is a sample of a dictionary entry for the word **key**.

> **Key** /ki/ n., pl. keys, adj., v., keyed, keyring **1.** an instrument for fastening or opening a lock. **2.** a means of understanding, solving etc.: *the key to a problem.* **3.** a book or the like containing the solutions or translations of material. **4.** the system or pattern used to decode. **5.** an explanation of symbols used on a map etc. **6.** one of a set of buttons or levers pushed to operate a typewriter, keyboard, piano etc. **7.** tone or pitch **8.** (mus.) system of related notes. **9.** (bldg.) To prepare a surface by grooving, roughening etc. to receive paint. [ME key(e), kay(e) OF kei, kai]

The entry word (**Key**) shows how to spell the word.

Pronunciation (/ki/) shows how to say the word.

Part of speech (n.) shows if the word is a noun, verb, adjective etc.

Definition (1.–9.) shows the meanings of the word.

Usage (*the key to a problem*) shows how to use the word in a sentence.

Word origin ([ME—Middle English]) shows where the word comes from.

Answers

Note: dictionary and thesaurus examples may vary.

1. (a) 9
   (c) keys
   (e) system of related notes
   (g) the key to a problem
   (i) kettle
   (b) noun
   (d) keyed, keying
   (f) key/keye, kay/kaye and kei/kai
   (h) building trade
   (j) Sentences will vary.

2. (a) judge—a public officer authorised to determine causes in a court of law, to form an opinion
   (b) condition—an existing state *(What condition is it in?)*, something demanded as an essential part of an agreement
   (c) exercise—physical activity, a written task
   (d) measure—the act of finding the size, dimensions, quantity etc. of something, a unit or standard of measurement

3. Answers will vary. (Nouns are naming words.)

Dictionary use

This is a sample of a dictionary entry for the word *Key.*

Key /ki/ n., pl. keys, adj., v., keyed, keyring **1.** an instrument for fastening or opening a lock. **2.** a means of understanding, solving etc.: ***the key to a problem***. **3.** a book or the like containing the solutions or translations of material. **4.** the system or pattern used to decode. **5.** an explanation of symbols used on a map etc. **6.** one of a set of buttons or levers pushed to operate a typewriter, keyboard, piano etc. **7.** tone or pitch **8.** (mus.) system of related notes. **9.** (bldg.) To prepare a surface by grooving, roughening etc. to receive paint. [ME key(e), kay(e) OF kei, kai]

1. **Use the entry to answer the following.**

   (a) How many definitions are given for the word? _____

   (b) What type of word is **key**? _____

   (c) Write the plural form. _____

   (d) Write two verbs formed from the word **key**. _____   _____

   (e) Write the musical definition given for the word. _____

   (f) The word originates from two old languages. Write a spelling from Middle English _____ and one from Old French _____.

   (g) Write the usage example given for the second definition. _____

   (h) In what trade does the last definition apply? _____

   (i) Which guide word is more likely to be at the top of the page for this entry?   **kettle**   **known**   **knock**

   (j) Write three sentences to show different meanings for the word **key**. _____

   _____

   _____

   _____

2. **Use a dictionary to find each word. Write two sentences to show different meanings for each word.**

   (a) judge _____

   _____

   (b) condition _____

   _____

   (c) exercise _____

   _____

   (d) measure _____

   _____

3. **Write six common nouns that all belong to one theme; e.g. holidays, art, music, computers. Use a dictionary to find each word and write the first definition given. Write the guide words located at the top of the page.**

Noun	Definition	Guide word

TEACHER INFORMATION

Many English words are derived from Latin and Greek words. See page xvii for a list of examples.

An **eponym** refers to a person who gives his or her name (usually last name) to words; e.g. **Jules Leotard** introduced a one-piece, close-fitting garment worn by acrobats and dancers. The word itself is also known as an eponym.

Many commonly used words in English are derived from other languages; e.g. **'siesta'** is a Spanish word for **'small sleep'**.

Answers

1. (a) transmit   (b) portable   (c) audience
   (d) manuscript   (e) microscope   (f) monolith

2. Possible definitions include:
   (a) periscope—an instrument used to view objects above a surface or eye level
   (b) manual—something done with the hands
   (c) audition—a trial hearing for an actor, singer etc.
   (d) export—send (goods) to another country
   (e) admit—to let in, allow entrance of, accept as valid, acknowledge, confess
   (f) monorail—a railway with carriages running on a single rail

3. Answers will vary. Examples: include:
   (a) auto (self)—autograph, automatic, automobile, autobiography, autodestruct, autocrat, autopilot
   (b) phone (sound)—telephone, phonic, phoneme, phonetic, phonogram, gramophone
   (c) graph (write)—autograph, graphology, geography, graphite, graphic(s), biography, photography, choreography
   (d) aqua (water)—aquarium, Aquarius, aquatic, aquamarine, aquaphobia, aquaplane, aqueduct, aqueous
   (e) dent (tooth)—dentist, denture, dentine, dental, dentistry, dentition

4. Write a word to match each of these descriptions.
   (a) hamburger   (b) champagne   (c) braille
   (d) siesta   (e) blizzard   (f) kangaroo
   (g) August   (h) Sunday   (i) umbrella

Word origins

Many words from other languages are used to form some of the English words we use today. Here are some words from the Greek and Latin languages and their meanings.

- *scope*—**from Greek, meaning** *to look or examine*
- *port*—**from Latin, meaning** *carry*
- *manu*—**from Latin, meaning** *hand*
- *mono*—**from Greek, meaning** *one*
- *aud*—**from Latin, meaning** *to hear*
- *mit*—**from Latin, meaning** *to let go or send*

1. **Write the correct word to match each definition.**

| *manuscript* | *transmit* | *monolith* | *portable* | *microscope* | *audience* |

(a) To send a communication to a person or destination. ....

(b) Something that is easily carried around. ....

(c) A group of people in attendance to hear a performance. ....

(d) A document written by hand. ....

(e) A magnifying instrument to examine small objects. ....

(f) A single piece of stone that is a large size and either natural or constructed. ....

2. **Write a definition for each of the following words.**

(a) peri<u>scope</u> _____

(b) <u>manu</u>al _____

(c) <u>aud</u>ition _____

(d) ex<u>port</u> _____

(e) ad<u>mit</u> _____

(f) <u>mono</u>rail _____

3. **Write four words for each of the following, which are all from the Greek language. The meaning is shown in brackets.**

(a) auto (self) _____ _____ _____ _____

(b) phone (sound) _____ _____ _____ _____

(c) graph (write) _____ _____ _____ _____

(d) aqua (water) _____ _____ _____ _____

(e) dent (tooth) _____ _____ _____ _____

4. **Write a word to match each of these descriptions.**

(a) A popular food from Hamburg in Germany. ....

(b) A sparkling drink from Champagne in France. ....

(c) A system of reading for the blind invented by Louis Braille. ....

(d) A Spanish word for a short nap taken in the afternoon. ....

(e) An American word that describes a violent snowstorm. ....

(f) An Aboriginal Australian word for a pouched animal that leaps on its hind legs. ....

(g) A month of the year named after the Roman emperor, Augustus Caesar. ....

(h) A day of the week named after an Old English word meaning *sun*. ....

(i) A useful item in the rain named after Latin words meaning *shade* and *little*. ....

PUPIL NAME

TEACHER INFORMATION

A **capital letter** is used:

- to start a sentence; e.g. **S**he is here today.

- for the pronoun **I**, including **I**'m, **I**'ve, **I**'ll and **I**'d

- as the first letter of a proper noun; e.g. **I**reland, **T**homas, **P**acific **O**cean

- to start direct speech; e.g. I said, '**S**he is here today'.

- for the initial letter and proper nouns in titles of books, films etc.; e.g. **B**lack **B**eauty, **F**inding **N**emo.

Prim-Ed Publishing® employs minimal capitalisation for titles of books and other publications, as recommended by the *Style manual for authors, editors and printers*, sixth edition, 2002.

Answers

1. (a) **J**ade and **I** walked down **V**alley **R**oad and across **S**tratton **P**ark to visit **A**lesha.
   (b) **JK R**owling wrote the **H**arry **P**otter books **I** borrowed from **B**eechwood **L**ibrary.
   (c) **S**ome of the **H**ollywood celebrities live in **B**everley **H**ills and **M**alibu, **C**alifornia.
   (d) **M**y dream is to travel to **E**urope, visiting **P**aris and **R**ome, and to go to **S**outh **A**frica.
   (e) The principal of **M**ount **S**treet **P**rimary **S**chool, in **O**akwood, is **M**rs **C**larkson.
   (f) The tourists from **N**ew **Z**ealand went to **C**able **B**each in **B**roome for the month of **J**uly.

2. Answers will vary.

3. (a) The **W**orld **C**up's final was held in **L**ondon at **W**embley **S**tadium, on 30 **J**uly. The match was played between **E**ngland and **G**ermany. The final score was 4–2, with **E**ngland winning through the efforts of **G**eoff **H**urst.

   (b) The accident happened at the corner of **S**outh **S**treet and **G**lenridge **R**oad in **R**iverstown. **P**aramedics from the **S**t **J**ohn **A**mbulance **S**ervice attended almost immediately. **W**hen police officers arrived from the **R**iverstown **S**tation, they realised the nearby **L**ockwood **F**ire **S**ervice would need to be involved. **B**oth cars were wrecked and one woman was trapped. **R**ose **C**ooper was one of the passengers who escaped with minor injuries. **T**he other two victims were taken to **R**oyal **P**erth **H**ospital for treatment.

   (c) **T**rent, **M**ax and **J**ake all played for the **R**angers **B**asketball **C**lub. **D**uring the season, they trained on **M**onday and **T**hursday from 4.00 to 5.30 pm. **T**heir games were usually played on a **S**aturday morning, with the older kids playing in the afternoon. **J**ake's dad, **M**r **W**illiams, took the boys to training on **M**onday's and helped the coach. **O**n **T**hursdays, **M**rs **S**cott made sure everyone made it to training on time. **A**bout once a month, the three families got together for a barbecue after the **S**aturday game.

Capital letters

1. Show where the capital letters should be in each sentence.

(a) jade and i walked down valley road and across stratton park to visit alesha.

(b) jk rowling wrote the harry potter books I borrowed from beechwood library.

(c) some of the hollywood celebrities live in beverley hills and malibu, california.

(d) my dream is to travel to europe, visiting paris and rome, and to go to south africa.

(e) the principal of mount street primary school, in oakwood, is mrs clarkson.

(f) the tourists from new zealand went to cable beach in broome for the month of july.

2. All proper nouns need a capital letter. Complete these sentences by adding proper nouns.

(a) The school I attend is _____.

(b) _____ is the most famous landmark in _____.

(c) My friend _____ enjoys watching _____.

(d) _____ is the computer program I use most often.

(e) The _____ is a charity that I support.

(f) I think that the most famous place in _____ is _____.

3. Show where the capital letters should be in each paragraph.

(a) the world cup's final was held in london at wembley stadium, on 30 july. the match was played between england and germany. the final score was 4–2, with england winning through the efforts of geoff hurst.

(b) the accident happened at the corner of south street and glenridge road in riverstown. paramedics from the st john ambulance service attended almost immediately. when police officers arrived from the riverstown station, they realised the nearby lockwood fire service would need to be involved. both cars were wrecked and one woman was trapped. rose cooper was one of the passengers who escaped with minor injuries. the other two victims were taken to royal perth hospital for treatment.

(c) trent, max and jake all played for the rangers basketball club. during the season, they trained on monday and thursday from 4.00 to 5.30 pm. their games were usually played on a saturday morning, with the older kids playing in the afternoon. jake's dad, mr williams, took the boys to training on monday's and helped the coach. on thursdays, mrs scott made sure everyone made it to training on time. about once a month, the three families got together for a barbecue after the saturday game.

TEACHER INFORMATION

A **full stop** (.) is used:

- to show the end of a statement; e.g. She went to school.

- for abbreviations when only the first part of the word is used; e.g. Feb., Capt.

A **question mark** (?) is used:

- at the end of a sentence that asks a question; e.g. How are you?

- in direct and reported speech where a question is asked; e.g. 'How are you?' she asked.

An **exclamation mark** (!) is used to show a strong feeling; e.g. That's brilliant! Ouch!

Answers

1. (a) Do you realise there are only three more weeks until the end of term?
   (b) Mum said she was really disappointed that she'd scratched her new car.
   (c) I'm too tired, so just leave me alone!
   (d) I'm going to ask her if she'd be interested in joining our netball team.
   (e) What do you think you might do with the money you've managed to save?
   (f) I was in the kitchen when my aunt suddenly yelled, 'Don't touch that!'

2. Statements will vary.

3. Questions will vary.

4. Exclamations will vary.

5. (a) 'Stop yelling at me! I won't listen if you can't speak properly. What's wrong with you, anyway?'
   (b) She asked if she could go to Mia's house. 'I'll be home by 5. That's a promise!'
   (c) I went outside so I could read in peace. I couldn't believe it when the neighbour started the lawnmower!
   (d) I wondered what my brother was doing. I stood outside his door and listened. It was way too quiet!
   (e) The house we are buying is much bigger than this one. It even has a spa! I think we'll be able to have just one room where we can all study and use the computer. Dad loves the huge garage! We're thinking about creating a vegetable garden. I've already asked if we can plant strawberries.

Sentence endings

A complete sentence can end with a *full stop*, *question mark* **or** *exclamation mark*.

1. Write a *full stop*, *question mark* **or** *exclamation mark* **at the end of each of these.**

   (a) Do you realise there are only three more weeks until the end of term __

   (b) Mum said she was really disappointed that she'd scratched her new car __

   (c) I'm too tired, so just leave me alone __

   (d) I'm going to ask her if she'd be interested in joining our netball team __

   (e) What do you think you might do with the money you've managed to save __

   (f) I was in the kitchen when my aunt suddenly yelled, 'Don't touch that __'

2. **Write a statement about:**

   (a) your class _____

   (b) one of your talents _____

   (c) a place you've visited _____

   (d) your last birthday _____

   (e) your favourite pastime _____

3. **Write a question about:**

   (a) your favourite TV programme _____

   (b) something you would ask your parents _____

   (c) the country you live in _____

   (d) a person you would like to meet _____

   (e) something that's confused you _____

4. **Write an exclamation about:**

   (a) something that's scared you _____

   (b) a time you were angry _____

   (c) something that made you laugh _____

   (d) your greatest achievement _____

   (e) a celebrity _____

5. **Provide the correct endings.**

   (a) 'Stop yelling at me I won't listen if you can't speak properly What's wrong with you, anyway '

   (b) She asked if she could go to Mia's house 'I'll be home by 5 That's a promise '

   (c) I went outside so I could read in peace I couldn't believe it when the neighbour started the lawnmower

   (d) I wondered what my brother was doing I stood outside his door and listened It was way too quiet

   (e) The house we are buying is much bigger than this one It even has a spa I think we'll be able to have just one room where we can all study and use the computer Dad loves the huge garage We're thinking about creating a vegetable garden I've already asked if we can plant strawberries

TEACHER INFORMATION

A **comma** (,) suggests a short pause and is used to make meaning clearer by separating parts of a sentence. Use a comma to:

- separate items in a list; e.g. I took pens, pencils, paper and paints to the class.

- separate lists of adjectives; e.g. He is talented, smart, strong and mature.

- separate clauses in a sentence; e.g. If I see him today, I'll definitely tell him.

- separate words, phrases and clauses at the start of a sentence; e.g. Firstly, I'm not going!

- separate words that add extra information; e.g. Kylie, my best friend, is coming to visit.

- separate the carrier *(I replied)* from the direct speech; e.g. 'That is Kylie', I replied.

Answers

1. (a) Ella, Lucy and Olivia have been best friends since they first started school.
   (b) Friday is my favourite day because we have assembly, art, science and sport.
   (c) We went to the beach and surfed, swam, ate ice-cream and built a giant sandcastle.
   (d) Our family celebrates Christmas, Easter, birthdays and New Year's Day.
   (e) I wasn't happy when Mum decided not to buy muffins, pizza, cupcakes, chocolate and biscuits.

2. (a) Although the accident was serious enough to close the road, the emergency services worked quickly and no-one died.
   (b) The new government was elected in March, though some people weren't happy with the result.
   (c) I'm not really interested in watching that film, unless you've got plenty of popcorn to eat!
   (d) Tessa promised she would be absolutely honest, then she told me something I knew was untrue.
   (e) Unless I finish the jobs I need to do at home, I'm not going to be able to go out.

3. (a) Melbourne, in Australia, has wonderful sporting facilities.
   (b) I used my imagination, which is sometimes bizarre, to write an incredible story for the school paper.
   (c) Dad decided that his mobile phone, bought two years ago, was now obsolete.
   (d) The netball team I support, the Flying Eagles, finally made it to the grand final.
   (e) The new shoes my sister bought, which cost a small fortune, were so high I thought she might fall.

4. (a) My best friend, Jason, is a lot like me, except for the colour of his hair, which is black.
   (b) My computer, an old one, seemed to be working slower every day, though it could be my imagination.
   (c) Dad and I went shopping for boots, socks, a jumper and a scarf so that we'd be ready for the new season, which starts in a week.
   (d) The roast dinner, which Nan cooked, had potatoes, pumpkin, corn, parsnip and tender chicken.
   (e) If I can't see you on Saturday, I'll call, text or email to let you know what I'm doing.

5. When my parents bought their new high definition TV, they thought it would be easy to connect. However, it soon turned to frustration as Dad, who is always quick to temper, couldn't work out which cord went where. 'Read the instructions', Mum advised, but Dad didn't listen. It soon turned worse when Dad, looking triumphant, pressed a button and expected the screen to light up. Instead, a big spark flashed, a loud bang was heard and smoke started rising from the back of the TV. Oh no!

1. **Use a comma to separate items in a list.**

   (a) Ella Lucy and Olivia have been best friends since they first started school.

   (b) Friday is my favourite day because we have assembly art science and sport.

   (c) We went to the beach and surfed swam ate ice-cream and built a giant sandcastle.

   (d) Our family celebrates Christmas Easter birthdays and New Year's Day.

   (e) I wasn't happy when Mum decided not to buy muffins pizza cupcakes chocolate and biscuits.

2. **Use a comma to separate two or more sentences or phrases that are joined together.**

   (a) Although the accident was serious enough to close the road the emergency services worked quickly and no-one died.

   (b) The new government was elected in March though some people weren't happy with the result.

   (c) I'm not really interested in watching that film unless you've got plenty of popcorn to eat!

   (d) Tessa promised she would be absolutely honest then she told me something I knew was untrue.

   (e) Unless I finish the jobs I need to do at home I'm not going to be able to go out.

3. **Use a comma to separate words added for extra information.**

   (a) Melbourne in Australia has wonderful sporting facilities.

   (b) I used my imagination which is sometimes bizarre to write an incredible story for the school paper.

   (c) Dad decided that his mobile phone bought two years ago was now obsolete.

   (d) The netball team I support the Flying Eagles finally made it to the grand final.

   (e) The new shoes my sister bought which cost a small fortune were so high I thought she might fall.

4. **Show where the commas should be.**

   (a) My best friend Jason is a lot like me except for the colour of his hair which is black.

   (b) My computer an old one seemed to be working slower every day though it could be my imagination.

   (c) Dad and I went shopping for boots socks a jumper and a scarf so that we'd be ready for the new season which starts in a week.

   (d) The roast dinner which Nan cooked had potatoes pumpkin corn parsnip and tender chicken.

   (e) If I can't see you on Saturday I'll call text or email to let you know what I'm doing.

5. **There are too many commas in this paragraph. Use a delete mark (/) where required.**

   When my parents, bought their new high, definition TV, they thought it would be easy to connect. However, it soon turned to frustration, as Dad, who is always quick to temper, couldn't work out which cord, went where. 'Read the instructions', Mum advised, but Dad didn't listen. It soon turned worse, when Dad, looking triumphant, pressed a button and, expected the screen to light up. Instead, a big spark flashed, a loud bang was heard, and smoke started rising, from the back of the TV. Oh, no!

PUPIL NAME

TEACHER INFORMATION

Quotation marks (' ') are used to:

- enclose direct speech; e.g. 'I can see you', said Tim.

- show quotations within quotations; e.g. 'The song is called "Insects"', I think', said Maya.

- enclose words that the writer may not be using in their usual sense; e.g. The learner driver 'kangaroo-hopped' down the road.

- enclose the meaning of a word; e.g. The Spanish word 'siesta' means 'a short nap'.

- enclose titles of books, songs, special names, plays etc. (in handwritten work); e.g. 'The lion king' was playing.

Prim-Ed Publishing® follows guidelines for punctuation and grammar as recommended by the *Style manual for authors, editors and printers*, sixth edition, 2002. Note, however, that teachers should use their preferred guidelines if there is a conflict.

Answers

1. (a) 'Are you going to celebrate your birthday this year?' Kelly asked Amber.
   (b) The teacher said, 'You will need to complete this work before lunch'.
   (c) Emma asked her cousin to come over and Alice said, 'Great! I'll be there soon'.
   (d) 'I don't really remember exactly what happened that day', the man told the officer.
   (e) His doctor stated, 'The condition is definitely not as serious as I first thought'.
   (f) 'Think about creating a quality piece that could be the centre of attention', suggested the artist.

2. (a) 'My parents are usually great,' said Jess, 'but yesterday they were both tired and grumpy'.
   (b) 'Our regular training has been cancelled,' I told Dad, 'so can I go to Max's for awhile?'
   (c) 'I'm so disappointed you've been dishonest, Tom', Mum said. 'There was no reason for you to make that choice.'
   (d) 'Take that man into custody immediately', ordered the judge. 'The jury has made its decision.'
   (e) 'A calculator will be available for the first test,' explained Mrs Lee, 'but not the second'.
   (f) 'We just passed a horrible car accident', I told Dad. 'I saw two ambulances, the police and a fire truck.'

3. (a) 'Mum said, "Be back at five o'clock"', I told Oliver's dad.
   (b) Zac said, 'I don't understand this. It's says here, "Write a complex sentence with adjectives "'.
   (c) 'Place your feet solidly on the blocks before the starter says, "Take your mark!"' the coach explained.
   (d) 'Did you actually say, "I haven't finished my homework yet"?' Mum asked.
   (e) 'I watched the film "Australia" last night and enjoyed it', Adam said to Trent.
   (f) 'The title is "Jane's promise" and it is printed at the top of each page', I told her.

4. (a) 'Do you exercise for 30 minutes every day?' I asked Aunt Amy.
   (b) The librarian said, 'You really need to keep the noise down'.
   (c) 'The price is expensive,' the repairer said, 'but if you pay cash, I'll charge 10% less'.

5. Answers will vary.

Quotation marks

Quotation marks **are used to show the exact words that someone has spoken.**

1. Show where the quotation marks should be.

(a) Are you going to celebrate your birthday this year? Kelly asked Amber.

(b) The teacher said, You will need to complete this work before lunch.

(c) Emma asked her cousin to come over and Alice said, Great! I'll be there soon.

(d) I don't really remember exactly what happened that day, the man told the officer.

(e) His doctor stated, The condition is definitely not as serious as I first thought.

(f) Think about creating a quality piece that could be the centre of attention, suggested the artist.

2. Use quotation marks to show the speech breaks.

(a) My parents are usually great, said Jess, but yesterday they were both tired and grumpy.

(b) Our regular training has been cancelled, I told Dad, so can I go to Max's for awhile?

(c) I'm so disappointed you've been dishonest, Tom, Mum said. There was no reason for you to make that choice.

(d) Take that man into custody immediately, ordered the judge. The jury has made its decision.

(e) A calculator will be available for the first test, explained Mrs Lee, but not the second.

(f) We just passed a horrible car accident, I told Dad. I saw two ambulances, the police and a fire truck.

Quotation marks **can be used for quotations within quotations. Different quotation marks are used for the 'inside quotation'. For example:** *'The book I read was "Twilight" and I'm looking forward to the film', I told Jake.*

3. Show the two sets of quotation marks in each sentence.

(a) Mum said, Be back at five o'clock, I told Oliver's dad.

(b) Zac said, I don't understand this. It's says here, Write a complex sentence with adjectives.

(c) Place your feet solidly on the blocks before the starter says, Take your mark! the coach explained.

(d) Did you actually say, I haven't finished my homework yet? Mum asked.

(e) I watched the film Australia last night and enjoyed it, Adam said to Trent.

(f) The title is Jane's promise and it is printed at the top of each page, I told her.

4. The quotation marks are incorrectly placed in each sentence . Write the sentences correctly.

(a) Do you exercise for 30 minutes every day? "I asked Aunt Amy."

_____

(b) "The librarian" said, 'You really need to keep the noise down'.

_____

(c) "The price is expensive, the repairer said," but if you pay cash, "I'll charge 10% less".

_____

5. Use quotation marks and write something:

(a) a pilot might say to his crew _____

(b) a customer might ask an assistant _____

(c) a boss might say to her employee _____

TEACHER INFORMATION

An **apostrophe** (') is used:

- in contractions to show where letters have been dropped; e.g. I've taken it. She's taken it.

- to show ownership with nouns in the possessive case, e.g. the boy's bag, the children's bags

- when parts of words are left out to show the way a character speaks; e.g. I like 'em.

When used to show ownership, the apostrophe is placed directly after the owner(s); e.g. a **lady's** hat, the **ladies'** hats, the **Smiths'** dog, Mrs **Jones's** cat.

Possessive pronouns—its, his, hers, ours, yours—do not use an apostrophe.

Answers

1. (a) Oscar's football match starts at 9 am on Sunday.
    (b) The teacher's computer was on a separate desk.
    (c) Hayley's artistic creation was displayed in the living room.
    (d) The room was a mess but at least Dale's bed was made.
    (e) The family photo is on the wall next to Mum's painting.
    (f) The teacher discovered that Emma's voice harmonised perfectly with Tim's.

2. (a) Jess's luggage was heavy so her dad carried it to the car.
    (b) Her parents' business employed eight other people.
    (c) The women's fitness club was an easygoing place to work out at.
    (d) Lucas's T-shirt was not appropriate in the restaurant's exclusive dining room.
    (e) The doctors held their meeting in the nurses' area so they could discuss the new patient's progress.
    (f) The ladies' room, men's room and parents' room were all newly decorated and the painter's work was excellent.

3. (a) The car's wheels had no tread.
    (b) The novel's title put me off.
    (c) The women's fashions were on display.
    (d) I heard the passenger's screams.
    (e) We heard the judge's words during the trial.
    (f) She asked about her husband's condition.

4. (a) Cody's work was terrific so he took it to the principal's office.
    (b) 'I haven't seen 'em anywhere', the old man told the officer.
    (c) We've read about the government's new policy and Mum's happy with the news.
    (d) I've listened to my neighbour's story and it's very interesting.
    (e) I couldn't believe the plumber's tools were left lyin' around.

Apostrophes

An *apostrophe* **is used to show ownership (***Lucy's dance***) and to replace missing letters when two words are contracted (***that's***). It can also be used when parts of a word are left out (***nothin'***) to show the way a character speaks.**

1. **Underline the owner and clearly show where the apostrophe should be.**
   For example: <u>*Tom's*</u> *party is today.*

   (a) Oscars football match starts at 9 am on Sunday.

   (b) The teachers computer was on a separate desk.

   (c) Hayleys artistic creation was displayed in the living room.

   (d) The room was a mess but at least Dales bed was made.

   (e) The family photo is on the wall next to Mums painting.

   (f) The teacher discovered that Emmas voice harmonised perfectly with Tims.

When adding apostrophes for ownership, the rule is that it is placed directly after the owner(s); e.g. The *men's* hats are blue. The *ladies'* hats are blue. *Chris's* hat is blue.

2. **Add apostrophes where they are needed.**

   (a) Jesss luggage was heavy so her dad carried it to the car.

   (b) Her parents business employed eight other people.

   (c) The womens fitness club was an easygoing place to work out at.

   (d) Lucass T-shirt was not appropriate in the restaurants exclusive dining room.

   (e) The doctors held their meeting in the nurses area so they could discuss the new patients progress.

   (f) The ladies room, mens room and parents room were all newly decorated and the painters work was excellent.

3. **Rewrite each sentence using an apostrophe where needed; for example:**
   The votes of the public are very important. *The public's votes are very important.*

   (a) The wheels of the car had no tread.   _____

   (b) The title of the novel put me off.   _____

   (c) The fashions of the women were on display.   _____

   (d) I heard the screams of the passenger.   _____

   (e) We heard the words of the judge during the trial.   _____

   (f) She asked about the condition of her husband.   _____

4. **Each of these sentences has missing apostrophes. They may be missing from ownership, contractions or where parts of a word are left out. Clearly show where they should be.**

   (a) Codys work was terrific so he took it to the principals office.

   (b) 'I havent seen em anywhere', the old man told the officer.

   (c) Weve read about the governments new policy and Mums happy with the news.

   (d) Ive listened to my neighbours story and its very interesting.

   (e) I couldnt believe the plumbers tools were left lyin around.

TEACHER INFORMATION

A *colon* (**:**) is used to introduce more information, which could be a list of words, phrases, clauses or a quotation.

For example: **Use the following: eggs, bacon, milk, salt and pepper.**

Answers

1. (a) (i)   There is only one word to describe that painting: brilliant!
       (ii) I could see two vacant seats: too close to the screen, though.
       (iii) Only four tickets for the five of us: not enough!
       (iv) I have two things to do: ironing and cooking.
   (b) Answers will vary.

2. (a) (i)   The book also had the following information: contents, index and glossary.
       (ii) Four pupils were elected: J Miller, K Newton, R Rogers and S Baker.
       (iii) The components are as follows: light, fire, air and water.
       (iv) He included the following: name, address, email and phone number.
   (b) Answers will vary.

3. Answers will vary.

4. Answers will vary.

Colons

A *colon* (:) is a punctuation mark used to introduce additional information.

A colon can be used to introduce a word or phrase that expands, summarises or illustrates what has come before; for example: *Only five tickets were available: not enough for our group.*

1. (a) Show where the colon should be in each of these sentences.

   (i) There is only one word to describe that painting brilliant!

   (ii) I could see two vacant seats too close to the screen, though.

   (iii) Only four tickets for the five of us not enough!

   (iv) I have two things to do ironing and cooking.

   (b) Write two similar examples, including the colon.

   _____

   _____

A colon can be used to introduce a series of items giving more information about what has come before; for example: *There were three subjects: Art, Music and English.*

2. (a) Show where the colon should be in each of these sentences.

   (i) The book also had the following information contents, index and glossary.

   (ii) Four pupils were elected J Miller, K Newton, R Rogers and S Baker.

   (iii) The components are as follows light, fire, air and water.

   (iv) He included the following name, address, email and phone number.

   (b) Write two similar examples, including the colon.

   _____

   _____

A colon can be used to introduce a dot-point series that provides more information. **For example:** *The pupils need to bring:*
- *warm clothes*
- *closed footwear*
- *toiletries.*

3. Write your own dot-point series to give information about the things you do to lead a healthy life.

   _____

   _____

   _____

   _____

A colon can be used to introduce the subtitles of books, etc. For example: *English: learning punctuation.*

4. Create three book titles and their subtitles. Use a colon.

TEACHER INFORMATION

A **semicolon** (**;**) is stronger than a comma but not as strong as a full stop. It is used to:

- separate short, balanced and linked phrases or clauses; e.g. *I bought new shoes; they were on sale.*

- separate items in a list of phrases or clauses; e.g. *I need 12 pens, pencils and rulers; 24 books, 6 erasers and 2 bags.*

A **dash** (—) is used to:

- provide additional information; e.g. *I opened the gift—it was just what I wanted.*

- show that something is unfinished; e.g. *I'm not so sure—.*

A **hyphen** (-) is used to:

- join two or more words or word parts; e.g. *dark-blue, go-ahead.*

- clarify meaning; e.g. *re-signed a contract, resigned from the job.*

- form some compound nouns and adjectival phrases; e.g. *brother-in-law, She is a well-known poet.*

- write whole numbers and fractions; e.g. *twenty-one, three-quarters.*

Answers

1. (a) My brothers and I love Chinese food; my sister prefers Thai.
    (b) They bought bottled water; it was very expensive.
    (c) A hot day was forecast; similar to yesterday.
    (d) The books were written by JK Rowling; all were made into feature films.
    (e) The recipe needs 500 g of chicken, diced; 2 cups of raw vegetables, sliced; and the stir-fry sauce.
    (f) The booklist shows 4 lead pencils, red pens and blue pens; 2 files and packs of loose-leaf file paper; coloured pencils and felt pen; and an eraser and sharpener.

2. Answers will vary.

3. Answers will vary.

4. (a) long-ball   (b) re-enter   (c) re-signed
    (d) well-known   (e) six-part   (f) re-created

Semicolons, dashes and hyphens

> A *semicolon* **shows a pause that is stronger than a comma but not as strong as a full stop. It is used to separate two parts of a sentence that are linked in meaning; e.g.** *They met when they were teenagers; now they are married.* **It is also used to separate items in a list, when those items already use commas; e.g.** *The menu was carrot and potato soup; roast beef, vegetables and gravy; and chocolate pudding, with berries and cream.*

1. **Show where the semicolon should be.**

   (a) My brothers and I love Chinese food my sister prefers Thai.

   (b) They bought bottled water it was very expensive.

   (c) A hot day was forecast similar to yesterday.

   (d) The books were written by JK Rowling all were made into feature films.

   (e) The recipe needs 500 g of chicken, diced 2 cups of raw vegetables, sliced and the stir-fry sauce.

   (f) The booklist shows 4 lead pencils, red pens and blue pens 2 files and packs of loose-leaf file paper coloured pencils and felt pens and an eraser and sharpener.

2. **Add your own ending after the semicolon.**

   (a) Mum enjoys cooking a roast dinner; _____

   (b) I love playing hockey; _____

   (c) We went shopping for groceries; _____

   (d) Our family lives on a large farm; _____

   (e) The flowers in her garden were beautiful; _____

   (f) It was a disappointing experience; _____

> A *dash* **is used to provide additional information, especially when the statement and list are part of the same sentence; for example:** *Many pupils scored high marks — in particular James, Jessica, Holly, Chas and Mark.*

3. **Add your own ending after the dash.**

   (a) Teachers need these qualities—_____

   (b) Pupils need to follow these rules—_____

   (c) The children are involved in the following activities—_____

   (d) The popular singer released these songs—_____

   (e) The rescuers included the following people—_____

   (f) The condition of the house was as follows—_____

> A *hyphen* **is used to join words and word parts (**e-book**), make a word clearer (**re-cover **instead of** recover**), create an adjectival phrase (**a much-loved book**) and divide a word at the end of a line.**

4. **Write the word that needs a hyphen.**

   (a) They need to kick less long ball shots.   _____

   (b) The workers were able to reenter the building.   _____

   (c) The netball star resigned with her club for another three years.   _____

   (d) She was a well known celebrity who often worked with charities.   _____

   (e) It was a six part television series that I really enjoyed watching.   _____

   (f) The artist recreated a painting that was very similar to the original.   _____

PUPIL NAME

TEACHER INFORMATION

Brackets are used to enclose additional information such as a comment, example or explanation. There are different types of brackets:

- Parentheses, or round brackets **( )** are often used to enclose extra information that is less important than the rest of the sentence; e.g. *Tia (my sister) showed me how to use the program.* A comma or dash is used if the extra information is just as important.

- square brackets **[ ]** are used to enclose extra information that is part of information already in round brackets; e.g. *The woman (Jane Doe [1962–99] of Wembley) wrote the book in Italy.* Square brackets are also used in written quotes when insertions are made by someone other than the original author.

- angle brackets **< >** are primarily used to enclose email and web addresses that are part of text, to lessen confusion with any other punctuation; e.g. *Contact <jdoe@mail.com> for details.*

- curly brackets **{ }** are most often used in more technical contexts; e.g. mathematical equations.

- slant or diagonal brackets **/ /** are most often used with web addresses.

An **ellipsis** (**...**) is three full stops used to show where letters or words have been left out; e.g. *Her birthday party was wonderful ... best ever!* An ellipsis can also mark a pause or interruption; e.g. *I just want to say ... Yes? What is it, Ali?*

The **forward slash** (**/**) is used:

- to show options; e.g. *yes/no*

- to show shortened forms; e.g. *a/c*

- instead of **per**, **an** or **a**; e.g. *40 km/h*

- in web addresses; e.g. *<www.prim-ed.com/books>*.

Answers

1. (a) The capital of the NT **(Northern Territory)** is Darwin.
   (b) The dress was made of white satin **(very soft)** and looked stunning.
   (c) We stayed up late to watch the action film **(on DVD)** on Friday night.
   (d) Our teacher said that only ten per cent **(three)** of our class failed to hand in their assignment.
   (e) Martha Harris **(1962–2004)** was a talented writer and painter who had two teenage children.

2. Examples include:
   (a) [Square]   The author wrote, I listen to RTM FM **[92.2]** , for the best music.
   (b) <Angle>   Contact the manager on **<j.doe@recruits.com>** for all the details.
   (c) {Curly}   The equation was **{3a x 4b}** + **{2a + 2b}** = 5a + 6b.
   (d) /Slant/   **/www.ww.com/** is the address.

3. Answers will vary.

4. Answers will vary.

5. Answers will vary.

6. Answers may include:
   yes/no   true/false   male/female
   he/she   p/a (personal assistant)   c/- or c/o (care of)
   40 km/h   www.numbers.co.zx/ten

Brackets, ellipses and forward slashes

Brackets are used to enclose additional information such as a comment, example or explanation. There are different types of brackets: parentheses, or round brackets ( ); square brackets [ ]; angle brackets < >; curly brackets { }; and slant or diagonal brackets / /.

Round brackets are often used to enclose extra information that is less important than the rest of the sentence; e.g. *Tia (my sister) showed me how to use the program.* A comma or dash would be used if the extra information is just as important.

1. **Use round brackets to enclose the extra information in each sentence.**

    (a) The capital of the NT Northern Territory is Darwin.

    (b) The dress was made of white satin very soft and looked stunning.

    (c) We stayed up late to watch the action film on DVD on Friday night.

    (d) Our teacher said that only ten per cent three of our class failed to hand in their assignment.

    (e) Martha Harris 1962–2004 was a talented writer and painter who had two teenage children.

2. **Find and write an example of how each of these brackets can be used.**

    (a) [Square] _____   (b) <Angle> _____

    (c) {Curly} _____   (d) /Slant/ _____

3. **Write three sentences that each include a different type of bracket.**

    _____

    _____

    _____

An *ellipsis* is three full stops (...) used to show where letters or words have been left out, for example: *Her party was great ... the best ever!* An ellipsis can also mark a pause or interruption.

4. **Add your own ending after the ellipsis.**

    (a) We had roasted chicken, vegetables and gravy ... _____

    (b) I downloaded four music tracks ... _____

    (c) The government introduced the new law ... _____

    (d) The forecast was a cold, rainy day ... _____

    (e) The patient's condition had become more serious ... _____

5. **Write a sentence where an ellipsis marks:**

    (a) a pause. _____

    (b) an interruption. _____

A *forward slash* (/) is used to show options and shortened forms, in web addresses and to replace certain words; e.g. *per* (km/h).

6. **Write examples for the different uses of a forward slash.**

Prim-Ed Publishing®   www.prim-ed.com

English – Back To Ba   *En*

Answers

1. (a) **L**eah used her mobile phone to call **J**essica and they arranged to meet on **S**aturday.
   (b) **D**id you know that one of the hottest months in **A**delaide, **S**outh **A**ustralia, is **M**arch?
   (c) **M**ax and **T**om were at **G**reenfield **P**ark when they saw **M**r and **M**rs **B**aker with their children.
   (d) **I** love that show! **M**y favourite characters are **M**organ, **K**irsty, **J**ay and **N**icole.
   (e) **I**'m sure **B**en's game finishes about 10.30, but can you please call **M**r **R**ogers and check?

2. (a) Mum and I bought invitations, balloons, streamers, banners and tinsel for Dad's party.
   (b) I used my computer, which is very slow, to download some information I was interested in.
   (c) The new television was purchased on Friday, though it wasn't delivered until Monday.
   (d) The doctor, who was just passing by, helped the two people involved in the accident.
   (e) We went to see the home which was for sale and noticed there were four bedrooms, two bathrooms, a large living room, a study and a two-car garage.

3. (a) 'Do you know how to stream these music tracks?' asked Belle. 'I can't work it out.'
   (b) 'If you do that again, you will be grounded', warned Dad. 'So make sure you don't go back there.'
   (c) 'The film "The Hulk" is about a superhero,' I told my brother, 'and I'm sure you will love it'.
   (d) 'I'm sure he specifically said, "Use the red one",' said Christie, 'but I think he's wrong'.
   (e) 'Write your name at the top of the page', the teacher said. 'Then write the title, "Punctuation".'

4. (a) My grandma's passion is gardening and she's always growing beautiful roses.
   (b) Mr Stewart's new car has amazing features and he's planning to take a trip that'll last a month.
   (c) I'm really not sure who's coming but I hope Jess's mum will bring her so there's someone my age.
   (d) Our parents' room needs painting, so they'll move to Chris's room until the painter's job is finished.
   (e) They listened to the community's concerns and said they'll meet again with the council's leaders.

5. **M**y close friend, **M**itchell **L**yons, was injured when his sister's car was involved in an accident. 'Thank goodness he had his seatbelt on!' I said. 'His injuries could have been much worse. He's still recovering but there're positive signs he'll be walking soon.'

6. The popstar's music was great **b**ut she's more famous for her outrageous behaviour! I think her fame must have changed her. She's probably not going to release another hit until she calms down. The concert's promoter isn't sure if she's even coming to **I**reland now.

1. **Use capital letters and the correct sentence endings to edit these.**

   (a) leah used her mobile phone to call jessica and they arranged to meet on saturday

   (b) did you know that one of the hottest months in adelaide, south australia, is march

   (c) max and tom were at greenfield park when they saw mr and mrs baker with their children

   (d) i love that show my favourite characters are morgan, kirsty, jay and nicole

   (e) i'm sure ben's game finishes about 10.30, but can you please call mr rogers and check

2. **Clearly mark where the commas should be in each sentence.**

   (a) Mum and I bought invitations balloons streamers banners and tinsel for Dad's party.

   (b) I used my computer which is very slow to download some information I was interested in.

   (c) The new television was purchased on Friday though it wasn't delivered until Monday.

   (d) The doctor who was just passing by helped the two people involved in the accident.

   (e) We went to see the home which was for sale and noticed there were four bedrooms two bathrooms a large living room a study and a two-car garage.

3. **Clearly mark where the quotation marks should be in each sentence.**

   (a) Do you know how to stream these music tracks? asked Belle. I can't work it out.

   (b) If you do that again, you will be grounded, warned Dad. So make sure you don't go back there.

   (c) The film The Hulk is about a superhero, I told my brother, and I'm sure you will love it.

   (d) I'm sure he specifically said, Use the red one, said Christie, but I think he's wrong.

   (e) Write your name at the top of the page, the teacher said. Then write the title, Punctuation.

4. **Clearly mark where the apostrophes should be.**

   (a) My grandmas passion is gardening and shes always growing beautiful roses.

   (b) Mr Stewarts new car has amazing features and hes planning to take a trip thatll last a month.

   (c) Im really not sure whos coming but I hope Jesss mum will bring her so theres someone my age.

   (d) Our parents room needs painting, so theyll move to Chriss room until the painters job is finished.

   (e) They listened to the communitys concerns and said theyll meet again with the councils leaders.

5. **Use your editing skills to correct this passage.**

   my close friend mitchell lyons was injured when his sisters car was involved in an accident thank goodness he had his seatbelt on i said his injuries could have been much worse hes still recovering but therere positive signs hell be walking soon

   _____

   _____

   _____

6. **The punctuation in this passage is all wrong. Rewrite the sentences correctly.**

   the Popstars music - was great But shes more famous for: her outrageous behaviour? "I think her fame, must have changed" her, shes probably not going to release … another hit: until she calms down the concerts promoter! isnt sure if shes even coming to ireland now?

   _____

   _____

   _____

TEACHER INFORMATION

Nouns are naming words. They name people, places, things and ideas.

Common nouns are words naming general rather than particular things; e.g. **apple, river, table, colour**.

Proper nouns name specific people and things and use a capital letter; e.g. **England, Luke**.

Collective nouns name a group of people, animals or things; e.g. **class, herd**.

Abstract nouns name an idea, concept or quality; e.g. **love, danger, youth, pain**.

Nouns are often identified by the placement of **a**, **an**, **the** or **some** in front of the word.

Answers

1.

Proper nouns	Common nouns	Collective nouns	Abstract nouns
London	neighbour	colony	beauty
Jack	parent	family	greed
Nile River	magazine	crowd	fear
New York	journal	team	truth
	property	orchestra	
	paragraph	swarm	
	chocolate	crew	
	kitten	alphabet	
	lunch		

2. (a) author, novels, year
   (b) judge, jury, evidence
   (c) holidays, police, safety, roads
   (d) calculator, measurement
   (e) brothers, courage, mother

3. Sentences will vary.

4. Questions will vary.

Nouns

Nouns are naming words. They name people, places, things and ideas.

Common nouns are words naming general things; e.g. *country, boy, pencil.*

Proper nouns name specific people and things and have a capital letter; e.g. *Australia, Kevin.*

Collective nouns name a group of people, animals or things; e.g. *class, herd.*

Abstract nouns name an idea, concept or quality; e.g. *love, danger, youth, pain.*

1. The following words are all nouns. Sort them into four different groups.

beauty	neighbour	parent	magazine	London	journal	Jack
family	crowd	property	greed	team	New York	orchestra	paragraph	fear
Nile River	chocolate	kitten	swarm	alphabet	lunch	truth	crew	colony

Proper nouns	*Common nouns*	*Collective nouns*	*Abstract nouns*

2. Write the nouns in each sentence.

(a) The respected author has published two novels in the past year. _____

(b) The judge asked the jury to listen carefully to all the evidence. _____

(c) During holidays the police are busy ensuring safety on our roads. _____

(d) The calculator was used to work out the exact measurement. _____

(e) The brothers showed a lot of courage when their mother was seriously ill. _____

3. Use these abstract nouns in a sentence. Underline the other nouns in each sentence.

(a) wish _____

(b) jealousy _____

(c) pain _____

(d) danger _____

(e) love _____

5. Write a question to which each of the following nouns is the answer.

(a) South Africa _____

(b) breakfast _____

(c) death _____

(d) choir _____

(e) government _____

TEACHER INFORMATION

A *verb* is a word or group of words that names an action or state of being. Verbs are often called 'doing words'; e.g. **read**, **walks**, **speak**, **has broken**, **ate**, **will type**.

Verbs can indicate tense, voice, mood, number and person.

Answers

1. (a) exercise
   (c) ask, wrote
   (e) predicted, would win
   (b) supplied, needed
   (d) separated, washing
   (f) remembered, put, was writing

2. Answers will vary. Examples include:
   (a) They **donate** money to the charity.
   (b) She **twisted** her ankle yesterday.
   (c) Dr Green **spoke** to the patient.
   (d) The politician **goes** to the meeting.
   (e) The lifesaver **rescued** the surfer.
   (f) The artist **created** a sculpture.
   (g) Rachel **called** her best friend.
   (h) Max's coach **trains** the team.
   (i) The couple **bought** a house.
   (j) The birds **made** their nests.

3. Sentences will vary.

4. Answers will vary.

5. Answers will vary. Examples include:
   (a) **write** carefully
   (c) **exercise** often
   (e) constantly **complains**
   (g) quickly **checked**
   (i) quietly **watched**
   (k) **spoke** yesterday
   (b) **act** properly
   (d) happily **plays**
   (f) recently **read**
   (h) easily **won**
   (j) **ran** hard
   (l) **snored** loudly

6. Answers will vary. Examples include:
   (a) athlete—trains, runs, swims
   (b) passenger—sits, watches, talks
   (c) parents—work, cook, discipline
   (d) branches—move, grow, die
   (e) neighbours—visit, meet, listen
   (f) surgeon—operates, washes, stitches, cares

Verbs

A *verb* is a word that names an action or state of being. All sentences need a verb with a subject;
for example: He (subject) *runs* (verb) to school.

1. Write the verbs in each sentence.

(a) My brother and I exercise every day. _____

(b) The teacher supplied her pupils with all the art materials they needed. _____

(c) Ask the doctor all the questions you wrote down. _____

(d) He separated all the white clothes from the others before washing them. _____

(e) He predicted the team would win by six goals. _____

(f) She remembered where she put the journal she was writing in. _____

2. Write a verb to complete each sentence.

(a) They _____ money to the charity.

(b) She _____ her ankle yesterday.

(c) Dr Green _____ to the patient.

(d) The politician _____ to the meeting.

(e) The lifesaver _____ the surfer.

(f) The artist _____ a sculpture.

(g) Rachel _____ her best friend.

(h) Max's coach _____ the team.

(i) The couple _____ a house.

(j) The birds _____ their nests.

3. Use each pair of verbs in a sentence.

(a) forgot, solve _____

(b) celebrate, opened _____

(c) study, achieve _____

(d) imagine, remember _____

(e) downloads, types _____

4. Write four verbs for each of these.

(a) things you do before school _____ _____ _____ _____

(b) things you do on a Sunday _____ _____ _____ _____

(c) things you don't like doing _____ _____ _____ _____

(d) things you would never do _____ _____ _____ _____

(e) things you enjoy doing _____ _____ _____ _____

(f) skills you have _____ _____ _____ _____

5. Write a verb to match each of the words (adverbs) shown.

(a) _____ carefully

(b) _____ properly

(c) _____ often

(d) happily _____

(e) constantly _____

(f) recently _____

(g) quickly _____

(h) easily _____

(i) quietly _____

(j) _____ hard

(k) _____ yesterday

(l) _____ loudly

6. Write two verbs that show what each of these nouns might do.

(a) athlete _____ _____

(b) passenger _____ _____

(c) parents _____ _____

(d) branches _____ _____

(e) neighbours _____ _____

(f) surgeon _____ _____

PUPIL NAME

TEACHER INFORMATION

The *tense* of a verb is used to show the time at which the action of that verb takes place.

Most verbs are regular and follow the same pattern for the past, present and future tense. For example, with the verb **to jump**: **I jump**//**I am jumping** (present tense); **I jumped**//**I was jumping** (past tense); **I will jump** (future tense).

Irregular verbs are those that do not follow this pattern, particularly in the past tense. For example: **I rise (rose)**, **I teach (taught)**, **I mean (meant)**, **I win (won)**, **I do (did)**, **I begin (began)**.

An *auxiliary verb* helps to form the tense of a verb. The verbs **to be**, **to have** and **to do** are auxiliary verbs; e.g. **I have** *eaten*. The auxiliary verb used in the future tense is **will**; e.g. **I will** *eat*.

Answers

1. (a) predicted—past   (b) divide—present   (c) will describe—future
   (d) questioned—past   (e) solves—present   (f) is exercising—present
   (g) download—present   (h) created—past   (i) separates—present

2. (a) The weather **changed** and a storm **came** in.
   (b) He **did** the housework and **made** the dinner.
   (c) The expert **spoke** and **displayed** information.
   (d) We **paid** for the tickets and **went** to the concert.
   (e) I **wrote** an email and **told** her I **had bought** dessert.

3. (a) I **invited** my friends to the party but forgot to ask my cousin.
   (b) She is **studying** for the English exam before watching TV.
   (c) My brother **drove** me to the game and stayed until the end.
   (d) We **fried** eggs and sliced mushrooms for breakfast.
   (e) I **will phone** you tomorrow and I will tell you about my dance class.

4. (a) I wish my nanna **was** here.   (b) Where were you going?
   (c) If the school was nearer, I'd walk.   (d) They were surfing.
   (e) The house is for sale.   (f) Cats have a lot of freedom.
   (g) Our neighbours are going away.   (h) My friends have gone out.
   (i) Their mail is being collected.   (j) She always has the right book.
   (k) Everyone is asleep.   (l) The team **was** playing well.

Verb tenses

Verbs can be changed to show what is happening in the present, what happened in the past and what will happen in the future.

1. **Write present, past or future next to each verb.**

   (a) predicted _____   (b) divide _____   (c) will describe _____

   (d) questioned _____   (e) solves _____   (f) is exercising _____

   (g) download _____   (h) created _____   (i) separates _____

2. **Rewrite each sentence, changing the verbs to the past tense.**

   (a) The weather is changing and a storm is coming in.

   _____

   (b) He will do the housework and make the dinner.

   _____

   (c) The expert is going to speak and display information.

   _____

   (d) We'll pay for the tickets and go to the concert.

   _____

   (e) I will write an email and tell her I'll buy dessert.

   _____

3. **The verbs in each sentence are not written in a consistent tense. Rewrite the sentences, changing the first verbs.**

   (a) I invite my friends to the party but forgot to ask my cousin.

   _____

   (b) She is study for the English exam before watching TV.

   _____

   (c) My brother drive me to the game and stayed until the end.

   _____

   (d) We frying eggs and sliced mushrooms for breakfast.

   _____

   (e) I phoned you tomorrow and I will tell you about my dance class.

   _____

4. **A singular subject needs a singular verb and a plural subject needs a plural verb. Circle the correct verbs.**

   (a) I wish my nanna [was | were] here.   (b) Where [was | were] you going?

   (c) If the school [was | were] nearer, I'd walk.   (d) They [was | were] surfing.

   (e) The house [is | are] for sale.   (f) Cats [has | have] a lot of freedom.

   (g) Our neighbours [is | are] going away.   (h) My friends [has | have] gone out.

   (i) Their mail [is | are] being collected.   (j) She always [has | have] the right book.

   (k) Everyone [is | are] asleep.   (l) The team [was | were] playing well.

TEACHER INFORMATION

A *pronoun* is used in place of a noun to avoid repetition.

Personal pronouns refer to people. They can be singular or plural, subjective or objective, and may indicate gender. Examples are: **I, you, he, she, we, they, me, him, her, his, them, mine, hers, theirs, ours**.

Impersonal pronouns refer to everything but people. They can be singular or plural, subjective, objective or possessive. Examples are: **it, they, them, theirs**.

Relative pronouns refer to people and objects and connect clauses and sentences. They are used in the three cases:
*   subjective – **who, that, which**
*   possessive – **whose, of that, of which, of whose**
*   objective – **whom, that, which**.
Other examples of relative pronouns are **whoever, whomever, whichever** and **whatever**.

Demonstrative pronouns replace nouns and function in the same way as nouns in a sentence. They have no gender but are used in the three cases:
*   subjective – **this, that, these, those**
*   possessive – **of this, of that, of these, of those**
*   objective – **this, that, these, those**.
Other examples of demonstrative pronouns are: **other, such, same, former, latter** and ordinal numbers (**first, second** etc.)

Interrogative pronouns are used in asking questions. They include **who, whose, whoever** (used for people), and **what, which** and **whatever** (used for things).

Reflexive pronouns are used in sentences that contain verbs whose actions are directed toward the subjects of the verbs. Add the suffixes **–self** or **–selves** to the personal pronouns **my, your, him, her, our, them** and **one**.

Indefinite pronouns are words that refer to people or things without saying exactly who or what they are. Examples include **all, another, any, anybody, anyone, anything, both, each one, either, everybody, everyone, everything, few, little, many, more, much, neither, nobody, none, no-one, nothing, other, others, several, some, somebody, someone, something** and **such**.
Note: Some indefinite pronouns can also be used as determiners; for example: *I would like* **some** (indefinite pronoun). *I would like* **some** *apples* (determiner).

Answers

1. (a) she, they   (b) he, he   (c) they, they
    (d) she   (e) she, we, she   (f) we, they, us

2. (a) singular—I, mine   plural—theirs   (b) singular—she   plural—they
    (c) singular—you, him, he   plural—them   (d) singular—it, hers   plural—we, ours
    (e) singular—it, his   plural—us

3. (a) that   (b) which   (c) who   (d) when   (e) what   (f) where

4. (a) somebody   (b) both   (c) something   (d) anything   (e) each   (f) everything

5. (a) who   (b) what   (c) which   (d) whose   (e) who   (f) which

Pronouns

A *pronoun* is a word that takes the place of a noun.

1. **Circle the pronouns in each sentence.**

   (a) She celebrated her birthday with a friend and they had a party.

   (b) He tried to copy the document but he had to ask his dad for help.

   (c) They found the problem difficult so they asked for help.

   (d) The passenger reading a book hoped she would not be disturbed.

   (e) She needed to know if we were coming because she wanted to order the food.

   (f) We watched the magpies protecting their nest until they scared us away.

Personal pronouns **refer to people.** *Impersonal pronouns* **refer to everything else. They can be singular or plural.**

2. **Underline the pronouns in each sentence. Write each under the correct heading.**

   (a) I am sure that is mine and not theirs.

   (b) She assumed they had breakfast.

   (c) Can you ask him if he will call them later?

   (d) We think it must be ours and not hers.

   (e) It is his and doesn't belong to us.

Singular	Plural
_____	_____
_____	_____
_____	_____
_____	_____
_____	_____

Relative pronouns **refer to people and objects and introduce a clause; e.g. There is the person** *who* **won the race. Relative pronouns include:** *who, which, that, what, when, where* **and** *why.*

3. **Use the correct pronoun to complete each sentence.**

   (a) The house _____ I live in has three bedrooms.

   (b) Select the animal _____ you prefer.

   (c) There are not enough roles for actors _____ are older.

   (d) Is there a time _____ you can come over to visit?

   (e) I think you know _____ you should do.

   (f) I travelled to a place _____ the scenery was beautiful.

4. **Write the indefinite pronoun in each sentence.**

   (a) I wish somebody would call.   _____

   (b) Both are going out.   _____

   (c) Something is going on that I'm not sure about. _____

   (d) I don't have anything to do this afternoon.   _____

   (e) Each will receive an achievement award.   _____

   (f) I love everything—especially my comfortable bed. _____

Indefinite pronouns **are words that refer to people or things without saying exactly who or what they are; e.g.** *Some* **were there.** *None* **was there.** *All* **were there.** *Few* **were there.** *Many* **were there.**

Interrogative pronouns **are words used to ask questions. They include** *who* **and** *whose* **(used for people) and** *what* **and** *which* **(used for things).**

5. **Use the correct pronoun to complete each sentence.**

   (a) _____ is your favourite television personality?   (b) _____ do you imagine is the best thing to do?

   (c) In _____ month of the year is your birthday?   (d) _____ toothbrush is that on the floor?

   (e) _____ is the author of the book you're reading?   (f) _____ option did you select?

TEACHER INFORMATION

An *adjective* is a word that describes or gives more information about a noun or pronoun; e.g. **pretty, thin, tall, delicious**. It qualifies the word it describes by making it more specific; e.g. *the* **red** *dress*—the adjective **red** specifies the colour of the noun *dress*. Adjectives can tell about the colour, size, number, classification or quality of a noun or pronoun. They can come before or after the noun and usually after the pronoun; e.g. *the* **beautiful** *bird, The bird is* **beautiful**. *It is* **beautiful**.

There are three forms of adjectives: absolute (e.g. **small**), comparative (e.g. **smaller**), superlative (e.g. **smallest**).

Answers

1. (a) red journal, old book   (b) large house, black roof
   (c) day-awful, horrible headache   (d) senior choir, national anthem
   (e) history test, perfect mark

2. Answers will vary. Examples include:
   (a) accident—terrible, frightening   (b) uniform—standard, green
   (c) wedding—extravagant, beautiful   (d) gardener—old, dedicated
   (e) chocolate—delicious, smooth   (f) passenger—young, talkative
   (g) traffic—slow, congested   (h) concert—fantastic, boring

3. (a) sourer   (b) gentlest   (c) more modern
   (d) most careless   (e) grander   (f) more, most

4. Answers will vary. Comparative and superlative forms are:
   (a) sweeter, sweetest   (b) wealthier, wealthiest
   (c) more polite, most polite   (d) huger, hugest
   (e) more musical, most musical

5. (a) The anxious girl asked the principal for assistance.
   (b) The beautiful dress looked stunning on the younger woman.
   (c) The Italian language was taught by a specialist teacher.

Adjectives

Adjectives **are words that describe or give more information about a noun or pronoun. They can tell something about the quality, characteristic, colour or size. You can identify an adjective by looking at the noun and asking, 'What's it like?'**

1. **Write the nouns and matching adjectives in each sentence.**

   (a) The red journal was located under the old book. _____ _____

   (b) The large house with the black roof is ours. _____ _____

   (c) My day was awful because of the horrible headache I had. _____ _____

   (d) The senior choir sang our national anthem. _____ _____

   (e) We did a history test and I achieved a perfect mark. _____ _____

2. **Write two adjectives for each noun.**

   (a) accident _____ _____   (b) uniform _____ _____

   (c) wedding _____ _____   (d) gardener _____ _____

   (e) chocolate _____ _____   (f) passenger _____ _____

   (g) traffic _____ _____   (h) concert _____ _____

   Adjectives can be used to make comparisons. Many comparative adjectives use *er* **or** *est,* **for example: young, young***er,* **young***est.* **Others need** *more* **or** *most* **added; for example: famous,** *more* **famous,** *most* **famous. A few words change altogether, for example: good,** *better, best.*

3. **Complete each sentence by modifying the adjective given.**

   (a) *(sour)*   The lemon is _____ than the grapefruit I tasted.

   (b) *(gentle)*   The _____ person I have ever met is my grandmother.

   (c) *(modern)*   My friend's family bought a television that is _____ than ours.

   (d) *(careless)* When it comes to checking my work, I can be the _____ person in class.

   (e) *(grand)*   The epic film was _____ than the last one we watched.

   (f) *(many)*   Dave has _____ games than I do, but James has the _____.

4. **Write a sentence using the adjective given to compare two or more things.**

   (a) sweet   _____

   (b) wealthy   _____

   (c) polite   _____

   (d) huge   _____

   (e) musical   _____

5. **The adjectives in these sentences are not placed close enough to the nouns. Rewrite each correctly; e.g. The child who was** *happy* **was with the lady. The** *happy* **child was with the lady.**

   (a) The girl who was anxious asked the principal for assistance.

   _____

   (b) The dress that was beautiful looked stunning on the woman who was younger.

   _____

   (c) The language that is Italian was taught by a teacher who was a specialist.

   _____

TEACHER INFORMATION

An **adverb** can modify or add information about verbs (e.g. *work* **quickly**), adjectives (e.g. **extremely** *pretty*) and other adverbs (e.g. *walking* **very quickly**). They indicate when (**soon**), where (**here**), how (**silently**) and how often (**frequently**). Many adverbs end in **ly**; e.g. *carefully, finally, nightly, exactly*.

Adverbs can be categorised as:

- time – again, early, now, never, often, then, today, tomorrow

- location – above, below, away, down, up, inside, outside, here, there

- manner – fast, slowly, well, happily, creatively, politely, carelessly

- degree – almost, entirely, little, much, more, rather, too, very

- reason – so, why

- number – first, once, second, twice, third.

Answers

1. (a) calmly   (b) finally   (c) daily
   (d) recently

2. (a) anxiously   (b) awfully   (c) nationally
   (d) gently   (e) equally   (f) sincerely
   (g) musically   (h) instantly   (i) honestly

3. Sentences will vary.

4. Answers will vary. Examples include:
   (a) repeatedly misbehaving   (b) immediately spoke
   (c) excitedly called   (d) instantly rejected
   (e) politely asked   (f) barely walking
   (g) comfortably sleeping   (h) violently kicking
   (i) faithfully following

5. Time—early, regularly, daily, never, today, then, currently, soon, immediately
   Location—above, centrally, inside, below, there, up
   Manner—honestly, violently, politely, wearily, sincerely, anxiously
   Degree—very, entirely, possibly, almost, barely

6. Answers will vary. Examples include:
   (a) definitely interesting   (b) extremely heavy   (c) very important
   (d) totally strange   (e) incredibly angry   (f) quite little
   (g) always regular   (h) entirely wonderful   (i) rather delicious

Adverbs

An *adverb* gives more exact information, usually about a verb, and sometimes about an adjective or another adverb. Many adverbs end in *-ly* and most answer the questions: when? (time), how? (manner) or where? (place).

An adverb can be placed at the beginning, middle or end of a sentence; e.g. *Usually* I listen to music. I *usually* listen to music. I listen to music *usually*.

It is not always clear if a word is being used as an adverb until you see what work it does in a sentence; e.g. She works *carefully* (adverb). She is a *careful* worker (adjective).

1. **Circle the adverbs in each sentence.**

   (a) She calmly waited for her grandfather.   (b) They finally saw the puppy.

   (c) She had a routine that she completed daily.   (d) I was recently able to finish the book I was reading.

2. **Change these adjectives to adverbs.**

   (a) anxious _____ (b) awful _____ (c) national _____

   (d) gentle _____ (e) equal _____ (f) sincere _____

   (g) musical _____ (h) instant _____ (i) honest _____

3. **Write two sentences to show the adverb placed in different positions.**

   (a) truthfully _____

   _____

   (b) perfectly _____

   _____

   (c) accidentally _____

   _____

4. **Write a verb to match each adverb.**

   (a) repeatedly _____ (b) immediately_____ (c) excitedly _____

   (d) instantly _____ (e) politely _____ (f) barely _____

   (g) comfortably _____ (h) violently _____ (i) faithfully _____

5. **Adverbs can give information about time, location, manner or degree. Write theses adverbs in the correct category.**

early	regularly	honestly	above	immediately	violently	daily	centrally
politely	inside	never	wearily	below	possibly	almost	soon	today
sincerely	entirely	then	there	barely	currently	up	anxiously	very

Time (when)	Location (where)	Manner (how)	Degree (how much)

6. **Write an adverb to go with each adjective.**

   (a) _____ interesting (b) _____ heavy (c) _____ important

   (d) _____ strange (e) _____ angry (f) _____ little

   (g) _____ regular (h) _____ wonderful (i) _____ delicious

TEACHER INFORMATION

A *conjunction* is a word (or words) that connects words, phrases, clauses and sentences; e.g. **and, but, because, so, that.**

- Conjunctions used to join sentences of equal importance are called **coordinating conjunctions**; e.g. *I like apples* **and** *oranges.* They include **and, but, for, yet, or, as well as, both, so, therefore** and **nor**.

- Conjunctions used to join clauses are called **subordinating conjunctions**; e.g. *She was happy* **because** *I arrived.* They include **because, before, if, while, until, like, though, although, unless, as, since, where, whenever** and **wherever**.

Answers

1. (a) and
   (d) so
   (g) before
   (j) although

   (b) but
   (e) unless
   (h) or
   (k) whether

   (c) because
   (f) so that
   (i) so
   (l) after

2. Answers will vary.

3. Answers may include:
   (a) There is a difference between addition **and** subtraction.
   (b) I am going to practise more **because** I'd like to do much better.
   (c) You really need to brush your teeth **before** you go to bed at night.
   (d) He's going to create a sculpture **and/while/then/or** she will paint a landscape to complete the project.
   (e) On Sunday, we will eat at the restaurant **where** we always enjoy our meal.
   (f) The judges were pleased **after** they had watched all the contestants perform.

4. (a) or, because
   (c) but, although
   (e) if, but, so

   (b) if, or
   (d) since, or
   (f) neither, nor, unless, and

Conjunctions

Conjunctions **are words that join together other words, phrases and sentences.**

1. **Write the conjunctions in each sentence.**

   (a) I hope I can afford a DVD and popcorn. _____

   (b) I feel a little anxious but I'm sure I'll be fine. _____

   (c) We celebrated on Saturday because it was my birthday. _____

   (d) I'm not sure how valuable it is so I'll ask an expert. _____

   (e) You probably can't imagine unless you've actually experienced it. _____

   (f) I'm going to take the luggage downstairs so that you will be ready on time. _____

   (g) You should ask the neighbour before you cut that shrub back. _____

   (h) I'm not quite sure if I feel disappointed or if I'm just relieved. _____

   (i) We're all going camping so we will leave school early. _____

   (j) I'm usually an honest person although I have told some white lies. _____

   (k) I'm going to enjoy the experience whether you come with me or not. _____

   (l) After reading about the history of the place, I couldn't wait to visit it. _____

2. **Add to each sentence after the conjunction.**

   (a) We all laugh **until** _____.

   (b) My best friend enjoys dance **while** _____.

   (c) The condition of the house was awful **yet** _____.

   (d) Natalie is not into formal exercise **nor** _____.

   (e) The problem was difficult to solve **though** _____.

   (f) I'm not able to attend that concert venue **as** _____.

3. **These sentences have the wrong conjunction. Write a more appropriate one.**

   (a) There is a difference between addition or subtraction. _____

   (b) I am going to practise more unless I'd like to do much better. _____

   (c) You really need to brush your teeth if you go to bed at night. _____

   (d) He's going to create a sculpture since she will paint a landscape to complete the project. _____

   (e) On Sunday, we will eat at the restaurant so we always enjoy our meal. _____

   (f) The judges were pleased or they had watched all the contestants perform. _____

4. **Write all the conjunctions used in each sentence.**

   (a) I think she will choose Kyle or James because they are good athletes. _____

   (b) She might go after the game if her neighbour takes her or her mum arrives. _____

   (c) He said he didn't know but I think he does, although I could be wrong. _____

   (d) I can't predict what they will do since I don't know Alice or Cassie. _____

   (e) I won't go if you don't but it should be good so please think about it. _____

   (f) The staff decided that neither Charlie nor Kane should go unless their behaviour improved and they apologised. _____

TEACHER INFORMATION

Prepositions are words that show the relationship between two words or phrases in a sentence. They show the relationship between time and space and are always attached to a noun or pronoun; for example: *Tim walked* **to** *school. The cat was* **under** *the tree. I sat* **behind** *Max.*

Prepositions are usually short words such as **on, above, in, with, by, near, down, off** and **along**.

More complex prepositions include **instead of, apart from, ahead of, with reference to** and **in addition to**.

Answers

1. (a) in   (b) beneath   (c) off
   (d) above   (e) during   (f) down
   (g) through   (h) across   (i) about
   (j) after

2. (a) inside, at   (b) on, with   (c) in, until, in
   (d) to, with, after, from   (e) into, during, after, to

3. Sentences will vary.

4. Sentences will vary.

5. (a) I don't think you should go after her. Preposition
   (b) We had our meal and Jessie came after. Adverb
   (c) I'll find that game after I finish lunch. Conjunction
   (d) Following school, the after years were bliss. Adjective

6. Answers will vary.

Prepositions

> *Prepositions* **are words that show how one thing is related to another.**
> **A preposition can show position, direction and time.**

1. Circle the preposition in each sentence.

  (a) The litre of water was in the fridge.

  (b) Put the boxes beneath the bed.

  (c) Take your shoes off the chair!

  (d) The plane was directly above us.

  (e) What will you do during the day?

  (f) Bring that down the stairs.

  (g) Go through the timetable and check.

  (h) We need to drive across the bridge.

  (i) The story is about a small child.

  (j) Have a shower after you eat breakfast.

2. Write all the prepositions in each sentence.

  (a) The valuable watch was stored inside a safe at the local bank. _____

  (b) The government was elected on Saturday with a large majority. _____

  (c) I need to study in my room until dinner is ready in the dining room. _____

  (d) We often go to the park with Dad after he is home from work. _____

  (e) My parents travel into the city during peak hour after taking us to school. _____

3. Write a sentence for each of the two prepositions given.

  (a) aboard, below _____

  (b) for, during _____

  (c) over, under _____

  (d) beside, since _____

  (e) between, near _____

4. Prepositions can be more than one word. Write a sentence for each prepositional phrase.

  (a) in front of _____

  (b) according to _____

  (c) because of _____

  (d) as far as _____

  (e) apart from _____

5. Some words can be used as prepositions and other parts of speech.
   Identify the word *after* in each sentence and write how it is used.

  (a) I don't think you should go after her. _____

  (b) We had our meal and Jessie came after. _____

  (c) I'll find that game after I finish lunch. _____

  (d) Following school, the after years were bliss. _____

> *preposition*
>
>   *conjunction*
>
> *adjective*
>
>   *adverb*

6. Describe a room in your house. Underline all the prepositions you use.

_____

_____

_____

_____

PUPIL NAME

TEACHER INFORMATION

A *sentence* is a group of words that makes sense on its own. The main parts of a sentence are the verb and the subject of the verb. Other elements of a sentence include the direct object of the verb, an indirect object and modifiers such as adverbs and adjectives, phrases and clauses.

To identify:

- the **verb** ask, what action is being taken?

- the **subject** ask, who or what is doing the action?

- the **direct object** ask, who or what receives the action?

- an **indirect object** ask, who or what is receiving the direct object?

There must be a direct object to have an indirect object, which is always a noun or a pronoun. The indirect object comes before the object and—although not stated 'to' or 'for'—the indirect object is understood.

For example: He (subject) gave (verb) **me** (indirect object) the ball (object).

Modifiers affect the meaning of another word in some way by giving more information. They might describe, define or make a meaning more precise. A modifier can be one word or a group of words.

Answers

1.

	Sentence	Verb	Subject	Direct object
(a)	Liam ate apples.	ate	Liam	apples
(b)	Expensive paintings hang on the wall.	hang	paintings	wall
(c)	The neighbour watered our garden.	watered	neighbour	garden
(d)	A thief stole the new computer.	stole	thief	computer
(e)	Miranda typed a short email.	typed	Miranda	email
(f)	He dressed in a suit and tie.	dressed	he	suit and tie
(g)	The waitress served four customers.	served	waitress	customers
(h)	The woman studied an English course.	studied	woman	(English) course

2. (a) us   (b) her   (c) grandmother   (d) us
   (e) him   (f) me   (g) his patient   (h) our class

3. (a) new   (b) weekend   (c) recently   (d) broken
   (e) carefully   (f) main   (g) whole   (h) elite
   (i) first   (j) old

A *sentence* is a group of words that makes sense on its own. The main parts of a sentence are the *verb* and the *subject of the verb*. Other elements of a sentence include the *direct object* of the verb, an *indirect object* and *modifiers* such as adverbs and adjectives, phrases and clauses.

To identify the verb ask, *what action is being taken?* Ask, *who or what?* to identify the subject. Ask, *who or what receives the action?* to identify the direct object.

1. Write the verb, subject and direct object in each sentence.

	Sentence	Verb	Subject	Direct object
(a)	Liam ate apples.			
(b)	Expensive paintings hang on the wall.			
(c)	The neighbour watered our garden.			
(d)	A thief stole the new computer.			
(e)	Miranda typed a short email.			
(f)	He dressed in a suit and tie.			
(g)	The waitress served four customers.			
(h)	The woman studied an English course.			

2. Write the indirect object in each sentence.

(a) Mr Jones showed us his paintings. _____

(b) The bride's father gave her some furniture. _____

(c) They took grandmother some cakes. _____

(d) The author offered us a signed book. _____

(e) The Red Cross gave him a certificate. _____

(f) My grandparents brought me the old photos. _____

(g) The doctor asked his patient a question. _____

(h) Our librarian told our class the rules. _____

> An *indirect object* is a noun or pronoun that tells who or what is receiving the direct object.
>
> For example: *Mum cooked us dinner. Mum* **is the subject,** *cooked* **is the verb,** *dinner* **is the direct object and** *us* **is the indirect object.**

> *Modifiers* **affect the meaning of another word in some way by giving more information. They might describe, define or make a meaning more precise. A modifier can be one word or a group of words.**
>
> **For example:** *He walked slowly.* **The verb** *walked* **is made more precise (modified) by adding** *slowly* **(adverb).** *The black dress suited the woman.* **The subject** *dress* **is described (modified) by adding** *black* **(adjective).**

3. Write the modifiers in each sentence.

(a) I used the new computer. _____

(b) Our weekend newspaper is delivered. _____

(c) We have recently returned. _____

(d) We threw out the broken chairs. _____

(e) He opened the present carefully. _____

(f) The TV is in the main room. _____

(g) The whole house was flooded. _____

(h) The elite athlete was injured. _____

(i) He lives in the first apartment. _____

(j) My grandfather has an old car. _____

TEACHER INFORMATION

A *phrase* is a group of two or more words that does not contain a verb and its subject. It does not make sense on its own. For example: **She walked towards the house.** **Towards the house** is the phrase of this sentence. It gives more information, or modifies the verb **walked**. **She** is the subject.

A *clause* is a group of words that does contain a verb and its subject. It can be a simple sentence; e.g. **We had very little rain last month.**

There are two types of clauses:

- The *main or independent clause*, which can stand by itself and make complete sense; e.g. **I ate a salad sandwich.**

- The *subordinate or dependent clause*, which does not make sense on its own. it depends on the main clause for its meaning; e.g. **because I was hungry.**

Answers

1. (a) behind the building
   (b) to the cinema
   (c) on the computer
   (d) in the swimming pool
   (e) the video game
   (f) with stunning fabric

2. Answers will vary.

3. (a) My brother stayed home
   (b) I read through the magazine
   (c) I felt strong and healthy
   (d) the town was full of tourists
   (e) they used a calculator
   (f) Megan was swimming in the ocean

4. Answers will vary.

5. My next door neighbour has a huge brown dog which is usually friendly. One day, it jumped the fence while young children were nearby. In a panic, the owner rushed out, desperate to bring his dog back.

Phrases and clauses

A *phrase* is a group of two or more words that does not contain a verb with a subject; for example: *She walked toward the house. Toward the house* is the phrase of this sentence. It gives more information, or modifies the verb *walked. She* is the subject.

1. **Underline the phrase in each sentence.**

   (a) They walked behind the building.   (b) My parents took us to the cinema.

   (c) Her work was typed on the computer.   (d) They played in the swimming pool.

   (e) He enjoyed the video game.   (f) Belle's dress was made with stunning fabric.

2. **Add a phrase to the subject and verb given to create a complete sentence.**

   (a) Troy celebrated _____.

   (b) They experienced _____.

   (c) Hayley accidentally broke _____.

   (d) Five different bands played _____.

   (e) The passengers listened _____.

   (f) My favourite author read _____.

A *clause* is a group of words that does contain a verb and its subject. There are two types of clauses:
   * The *main or independent clause*, which can stand by itself and make complete sense.
   * The *subordinate or dependent clause*, which does not make sense on its own. It depends on the main clause for its meaning.

3. **Write the main clause in each sentence.**

   (a) My brother stayed home because he was sick.   _____

   (b) I read through the magazine while waiting for the doctor.   _____

   (c) After I exercised, I felt strong and healthy.   _____

   (d) Before the bushfire, the town was full of tourists. _____

   (e) To solve the problem, they used a calculator.   _____

   (f) Megan was swimming in the ocean, unaware of the dangerous rip.   _____

4. **Write a dependent clause to create a complete sentence.**

   (a) Rose described the scene_____.

   (b) She measured the distance_____.

   (c) Kasey and Tara practised a routine_____.

   (d) _____ he answered the question correctly.

   (e) _____ we ordered a main meal and dessert.

   (f) The witness identified the suspect _____.

5. **Write a paragraph with three complete sentences using only these jumbled phrases and clauses.**
   the owner rushed out   which is usually friendly   My next door neighbour   desperate to bring his dog back
   In a panic   has a huge brown dog   One day, it jumped the fence   while young children were nearby

   _____

   _____

   _____

PUPIL NAME

TEACHER INFORMATION

A *simple sentence* has one main idea and usually contains only one verb and one subject. It cannot be broken down into other clauses; e.g. **Mark** (subject) **threw** (verb) **the ball** is an example of a simple sentence.

A *compound sentence* has two (or more) independent clauses with a conjunction.

For example, *Tim and I saw the film* **but I didn't enjoy it**.

Clauses can also be separated by a comma, semicolon or colon.

A *complex sentence* has a main (independent) clause and at least one subordinate (dependent) clause; e.g. *The doctor worked long hours at a hospital* **where there were many very sick children**.

Answers

1. Answers may vary.
   (a) Olivia is quietly reading in her own room until she goes to sleep.
   (b) Max hungrily ate the chocolate muffin which his mum had made.
   (c) The chef proudly cooked a sensational meal for the visiting celebrity to enjoy.
   (d) Lee happily watched a favourite film while it was raining outside.

2. Answers will vary.

3. (a) The actor entered the stage <u>while the lights were down</u>.   were
   (b) Please describe the suspicious character <u>that you saw as you left home</u>.   left
   (c) I love spending money <u>especially when the sales are on</u>.   are
   (d) The young man was rescued from the surf <u>when lifesavers paddled out on their surfboards</u>.   paddled
   (e) The family couldn't imagine living in the house <u>that wasn't near the beach</u>.   wasn't

4. (a) <u>I did some homework</u> while I waited for the bus.   past tense
   (b) After we played football <u>our coach made us all do three laps of the park.</u>   past tense
   (c) If the pool is going to be closed next week, <u>I will not be able to swim</u>.   future tense
   (d) <u>The school insists we all wear coats</u> when we go outside.   present tense
   (e) <u>My favourite uncle will be coming to see me play basketball next year</u> when he will be home from Canada.   future tense
   (f) <u>The flight attendant wants us to keep out seatbelts fastened</u> while there is clear air turbulence.   present tense

Sentences – Compound and complex

1. **Choose an adjective, adverb and clause from the list to expand each simple sentence. Write the new sentence.**

Adjectives	favourite	chocolate	sensational	own
Adverbs	proudly	hungrily	quietly	happily
Clauses	which his mum had made. until she goes to sleep.	while it was raining outside. for the visiting celebrity to enjoy.		

(a) Olivia is reading in her room _____

_____ .

(b) Max ate the muffin _____

_____ .

(c) The chef cooked a meal _____

_____ .

(d) Lee watched a film _____

_____ .

2. **Add a conjunction and another simple sentence to create a compound sentence.**

(a) The manager spoke to his employees _____ .

(b) The accountant calculated the difference _____ .

(c) My parents couldn't afford it _____ .

(d) The judge turned to the jury _____ .

(e) The government was elected _____ .

> A *complex sentence* **is made up of two clauses which both have a verb.**
> **One part of a complex sentence is dependent on the other.**

3. **Underline the dependent clause and write the verb it contains.**

(a) The actor entered the stage while the lights were down. _____

(b) Please describe the suspicious character that you saw as you left home. _____

(c) I love spending money especially when the sales are on. _____

(d) The young man was rescued from the surf when lifesavers paddled out on their surfboards. _____

(e) The family couldn't imagine living in the house that wasn't near the beach. _____

4. **Underline the main clause (the one that makes sense by itself), in each sentence and identify its tense.**

(a) I did some homework while I waited for the bus. _____

(b) After we played football our coach made us all do three laps of the park. _____

(c) If the pool is going to be closed next week, I will not be able to swim. _____

(d) The school insists we all wear coats when we go outside. _____

(e) My favourite uncle will be coming to see me play basketball next year when he will be home from Canada. _____

(f) The flight attendant wants us to keep out seatbelts fastened while there is clear air turbulence. _____

TEACHER INFORMATION

A *paragraph* is a group of sentences about one main idea. The sentences should follow in a logical order. It is usual to start a new paragraph when introducing a person, new place, change of time or idea.

Answers

1. (a) Paragraph should read:
    Emma and Aleisha asked for permission to download some music tracks. They promised they wouldn't spend too much. Aleisha wasn't quite sure which track to order first, so Emma chose her favourite. Both of the girls enjoyed the same style of music.

    Sentences not part of this paragraph are:
    Emma voted for the dance contestant on the reality TV programme.
    The popular band played at the music festival on Saturday.

    (b) Paragraph should read:
    The current government is preparing to release the annual budget. There are difficult times ahead for everyone in the country. Small businesses are finding it hard to afford their employees. Many people will lose their jobs. Some may even lose their houses. The Treasurer has forecast that taxes will rise and household expenses will increase. The best advice is to be careful about buying on credit.

    Sentences not part of this paragraph are:
    Our family will buy a new television tomorrow.
    My parents voted.

    Sentence incorrectly placed is:
    Some may even lose their houses.

    (c) Paragraph should read:
    The accident happened at the major intersection. Traffic from all directions was affected. The emergency services arrived quickly and took charge efficiently. Four cars were involved in the crash. A young woman was trapped in the smallest car and the firefighters were cutting it apart to reach her. The process took a long time. One paramedic was inside it, trying to keep the woman alive. Luckily, she was released in time and rushed to the hospital's emergency department. The police have yet to finish their investigation into the crash.

    Sentences not part of this paragraph are:
    I am not old enough to drive.
    The police cadets completed their training at the academy.
    His wife was a school teacher.

    Sentence incorrectly placed is:
    The process took a long time.

2. Individual answers required.

Paragraphs

A *paragraph* **is a group of sentences that are about one main idea. The sentences should follow in a logical order.**

1. **Identify and write the sentences that are incorrectly placed or should not be part of the paragraph.**

   (a) Emma and Aleisha asked for permission to download some music tracks. They promised they wouldn't spend too much. Emma voted for the dance contestant on the reality TV programme. Aleisha wasn't quite sure which track to order first, so Emma chose her favourite. Both of the girls enjoyed the same style of music. The popular band played at the music festival on Saturday.

   _____

   _____

   (b) The current government is preparing to release the annual budget. Some may even lose their houses. There are difficult times ahead for everyone in the country. Small businesses are finding it hard to afford their employees. Many people will lose their jobs. Our family will buy a new television tomorrow. The Treasurer has forecast that taxes will rise and household expenses will increase. My parents voted. The best advice is to be careful about buying on credit.

   _____

   _____

   _____

   (c) I am not old enough to drive. The accident happened at the major intersection. Traffic from all directions was affected. The process took a long time. The emergency services arrived quickly and took charge efficiently. The police cadets completed their training at the academy. Four cars were involved in the crash. A young woman was trapped in the smallest car and the firefighters were cutting it apart to reach her. One paramedic was inside it, trying to keep the woman alive. His wife was a school teacher. Luckily, she was released in time and rushed to the hospital's emergency department. The police have yet to finish their investigation into the crash.

   _____

   _____

   _____

   _____

2. **Use the sentence given to begin an interesting paragraph.**

   (a) Before I travel to France, I am taking some classes to learn more of the language. _____

   _____

   _____

   _____

   (b) I was immediately anxious when I saw the scene in front of us. _____

   _____

   _____

   _____

   (c) It was definitely the right time to celebrate! _____

   _____

   _____

   _____

PUPIL NAME

Answers

1. (a) proper noun   (b) collective noun   (c) abstract noun
   (d) common noun   (e) verb   (f) pronoun
   (g) adjective   (h) adverb   (i) conjunction
   (j) preposition

2. (a) present   (b) past   (c) future
   (d) future   (e) present   (f) past
   (g) future   (h) past   (i) present
   (j) future   (k) past   (l) present

3. (a) they, someone   (b) I, myself
   (c) she, somebody, nobody   (d) we, who
   (e) this, I, her, me   (f) we, ourselves, neither, us

4. Answers will vary. An adjective is a word that describes or gives more information about a noun or pronoun; e.g. *pretty, thin, tall, delicious*. It qualifies the word it describes by making it more specific; e.g. the *red* dress—the adjective *red* specifies the colour of the noun *dress*. Adjectives can tell about the colour, size, number, classification or quality of a noun or pronoun. They come before or after the noun or pronoun.

5. Answers will vary. A verb is a word or group of words that name(s) an action or state of being. They are often called 'doing words'. Verbs can indicate tense, voice, mood, number and person.

6. Answers will vary. Examples include:
   (a) position—under, down, near, over, across, inside, by, beside, above
   (b) direction—to, towards, from, through, around, across
   (c) time—during, after, before, past, since

1. **Write the word that identifies each of the following.**

   (a) Names specific people and things and always has a capital letter. .... _____

   (b) Names a group of people, animals or things. .... _____

   (c) Names an idea, concept or quality. .... _____

   (d) Names general people or things. .... _____

   (e) Names an action or state of being. .... _____

   (f) Takes the place of a noun. .... _____

   (g) Describes or gives more information about nouns. .... _____

   (h) Provides more exact information about other words and often ends in *ly*. .... _____

   (i) Joins together other words, phrases and sentences. .... _____

   (j) Shows how one thing is related to another. .... _____

2. **Write present, past or future to describe the tense of each verb.**

   (a) is celebrating _____   (b) argued _____   (c) will continue _____

   (d) will experience _____   (e) exercises _____   (f) disappointed _____

   (g) will measure _____   (h) positioned _____   (i) remember _____

   (j) will surround _____   (k) rescued _____   (l) judge _____

3. **Write the pronouns in each sentence.**

   (a) They told the officer their helmets were stolen by someone.   _____

   (b) I am going to sit by myself because their arguing is annoying.   _____

   (c) She wanted somebody to visit but nobody did.   _____

   (d) We saw the person who won the competition.   _____

   (e) This is difficult so I will ask her to help me.   _____

   (f) We are going by ourselves so neither of us need a lift.   _____

4. **Write a suitable adjective for each noun.**

   (a) graph _____   (b) alphabet _____   (c) magazine _____

   (d) community _____   (e) parents _____   (f) example _____

   (g) calculator _____   (h) government _____   (i) author _____

   (j) property _____   (k) mobile _____   (l) novel _____

5. **Write a suitable verb for each adverb.**

   (a) equally _____   (b) honestly _____   (c) anxiously _____

   (d) continually _____   (e) recently _____   (f) predictably _____

   (g) separately _____   (h) increasingly _____   (i) immediately _____

   (j) exactly _____   (k) perfectly _____

6. **Write four prepositions that indicate:**

   (a) position _____ _____ _____ _____

   (b) direction _____ _____ _____ _____

   (c) time _____ _____ _____ _____

Answers

1. New nouns may vary from those suggested.
   (a) I ate <u>chocolate</u> (**cereal**) for breakfast before my mum drove me to <u>Antarctica</u> (**school**).
   (b) Our family live in a four-bedroom <u>kennel</u> (**house**) with a <u>roller-coaster</u> (**pool**) outside.
   (c) The classical musicians played their <u>computers</u> (**instruments**) while the <u>Kelpie</u> (**audience**) listened.
   (d) The hive of <u>ants</u> (**bees**) knew their way around our <u>happiness</u> (**garden**).
   (e) My best <u>enemy</u> (**friend**) is travelling by <u>car</u> (**plane**) from New York to London.

2. (a) Ella is **exercising** at the gym where **her** friend often **goes**.
   (b) Tim and Zac are **sleeping** because **they** are **tired**.
   (c) He broke his finger and **asked her** to **take him** to the doctor.
   (d) They **purchased** a house and made **themselves** comfortable.
   (e) Aymee doesn't know if **anybody came** because **she** wasn't at home.

3. (a) She feels <u>best</u> (**better**) today than she did yesterday.
   (b) We bought the <u>cheap</u> (**cheapest**) bookcase we could find in the store.
   (c) Lighting a fire in the open is the <u>dumber</u> (**dumbest**) thing you could do on a hot day.
   (d) My cousin is <u>youngest</u> (**younger**) than me but my sister is the <u>younger</u> (**youngest**) of us all.
   (e) I chose the <u>thicker</u> (**thickest**) blanket because it is the <u>warmer</u> (**warmest**).

4. Answers may vary.
   (a) Her experience was so valuable <u>but</u> (**that**) the boss gave her a pay rise.
   (b) I needed to solve the problem <u>because</u> (**but**) I couldn't find my calculator.
   (c) You need to be honest about the accident <u>unless</u> (**so**) the doctor can treat you.
   (d) Ruby <u>or</u> (**and**) Jess are both going to the game <u>and</u> (**because**) they want to watch Elle play.
   (e) We will visit Paris <u>nor</u> (**or**) Rome first <u>only</u> (**and**) then go to Madrid.

5. Answers may vary.
   (a) I put the picture **of** my pet dog **on** the table **beside** my bed.
   (b) We swam **across** the river and played **on** the other side **until** we were ready to go back.
   (c) The crew were **aboard** the ship well **before** the passengers arrived **from** the departure room.
   (d) It was difficult to drive **during** the storm because the rain pounded **against** the windscreen.
   (e) I left home **without** any money so I turned **around** and went back.

1. **Underline the inappropriate nouns and write a more suitable word.**

    (a) I ate chocolate for breakfast before my mum drove me to Antarctica. _____ _____

    (b) Our family live in a four-bedroom kennel with a roller-coaster outside. _____ _____

    (c) The classical musicians played their computers while the Kelpie listened. _____ _____

    (d) The hive of ants knew their way around our happiness. _____ _____

    (e) My best enemy is travelling by car from New York to London. _____ _____

2. **Rewrite these sentences using the correct verb tense and correct pronoun.**

    (a) Ella is exercised at the gym where his friend often go.

    _____

    (b) Tim and Zac are sleep because themselves are tiring.

    _____

    (c) He broke his finger and ask she to taking his to the doctor.

    _____

    (d) They purchase a house and made yourselves comfortable.

    _____

    (e) Aymee doesn't know if nobody come because he wasn't at home.

    _____

3. **Underline the incorrect adjectives and write the word correctly.**

    (a) She feels best today than she did yesterday. _____

    (b) We bought the cheap bookcase we could find in the store. _____

    (c) Lighting a fire in the open is the dumber thing you could do on a hot day. _____

    (d) My cousin is youngest than me but my sister is the younger of us all. _____

    (e) I chose the thicker blanket because it is the warmer. _____

4. **Underline the incorrect conjunctions and write a more suitable word for each.**

    (a) Her experience was so valuable but the boss gave her a pay rise. _____

    (b) I needed to solve the problem because I couldn't find my calculator. _____

    (c) You need to be honest about the accident unless the doctor can treat you. _____

    (d) Ruby or Jess are both going to the game and they want to watch Elle play. _____

    (e) We will visit Paris nor Rome first only then go to Madrid. _____

5. **Complete the sentence by writing the correct prepositions.**

    (a) I put the picture _____ my pet dog _____ the table _____ my bed.

    (b) We swam _____ the river and played _____ the other side _____ we were ready to go back.

    (c) The crew were _____ the ship well _____ the passengers arrived _____ the departure room.

    (d) It was difficult to drive _____ the storm because the rain pounded _____ the windscreen.

    (e) I left home _____ any money so I turned _____ and went back.